CONSIDER YOUR CALLING

SIX QUESTIONS FOR DISCERNING YOUR VOCATION

GORDON T. SMITH

IVP Books

An imprint of InterVarsity Press
Downers Grove, Illinois

InterVarsity Press
P.O. Box 1400, Downers Grove, IL 60515-1426
ivpress.com
email@ivpress.com

InterVarsity Press® is the book-publishing division of InterVarsity Christian Fellowship/USA®, a movement of students and faculty active on campus at hundreds of universities, colleges and schools of nursing in the United States of America, and a member movement of the International Fellowship of Evangelical Students. For information about local and regional activities, visit intervarsity.org.

Scripture quotations, unless otherwise noted, are from the New Revised Standard Version of the Bible, copyright 1989 by the Division of Christian Education of the National Council of the Churches of Christ in the USA. Used by permission. All rights reserved.

While any stories in this book are true, some names and identifying information may have been changed to protect the privacy of individuals.

Cover design: Cindy Kiple
Interior design: Beth McGill
Images: Job finding icons: Stock vector © exdez/iStockphoto
Looking for talents icon: Stock vector © exdez/iStockphoto
Fitness icons: Stock vector © exdez/iStockphoto
Health icons: Stock vector © exdez/iStockphoto
Educational computer: Stock vector © exdez/iStockphoto

ISBN 978-0-8308-4607-8 (print)
ISBN 978-0-8308-9918-0 (digital)

Printed in the United States of America ♾

 As a member of the Green Press Initiative, InterVarsity Press is committed to protecting the environment and to the responsible use of natural resources. To learn more, visit greenpressinitiative.org.

Library of Congress Cataloging-in-Publication Data

Smith, Gordon T., 1953-
  Consider your calling : six questions for discerning your vocation / Gordon T. Smith.
    pages cm
  Includes bibliographical references.
  ISBN 978-0-8308-4607-8 (pbk. : alk. paper)
  1. Vocation--Christianity. I. Title.
  BV4740.S629 2016
  248.4--dc23

                                                                                    2015036052

P 17 16 15 14 13 12 11 10 9 8 7 6 5 4 3

Y 30 29 28 27 26 25 24 23 22 21 20

for joella

Contents

Introduction

What is the good work to which you are called? That is a good question, but it is not a simple question.

It is a good question because our work matters to us, to others and, of course, it matters to God. Indeed, the creator of the universe is the one who longs to give us good work—to call us into work that reflects the purposes of God in the world. Thus, it is a good question because work itself is a good thing.

For many, of course, work is sheer toil, with cruel and demeaning work conditions. But in that situation the problem is not work but the working *conditions*. Work itself is good. It is vital to our human identity, and we are most ourselves—most who God calls us to be, living in what it means to know the salvation of God—when we know the grace of work well done.

Indeed, we will only be happy—we will only flourish in the way that was intended when God created us—when we are doing good work. The goal of life is not less work but to know and embrace the good work to which we are called.

But while "What is the good work to which you are called?" is a good question, it is not a simple question. We are complicated souls and we live complicated lives. There is so much about daily life, our circumstances and the problems we face, that makes it difficult to make sense of the issues that intersect our lives. So many questions swirl through our minds as we encounter the inevitable transitions we have to navigate.

And we will navigate transitions. We hear different statistics all the time around the question of career changes. It would not be an overstatement to say that most of us will have a significant career and life transition every four to five years. We live in a fluid economy; the institutions of which we are a part are in constant flux. Our family situation changes, pressing us to consider what implications this has for our work.

And so, while it is a good question—it is complicated. And we do not wrestle with the question just once in life but rather as a regular part of living in a complex world. Therefore, surely, one of the basic capacities for living well is knowing how to navigate these transitions. Yes, there is the prior and ultimate question (What is the good work to which you are called?) but with that in mind, there are questions we can ask ourselves— questions that can help us make sense of these transitions and do so in light of the purposes of God in our lives. And that is the key: we want to approach the complexity of life and work through the lens of "vocation." We consider the calling of God on our lives and find clarity and purpose in life and work by coming at it all with a desire to know God and discern calling.

INTENTIONALITY

We easily view ourselves as "victims" of our circumstances, of what others have done for us and the ways they have, perhaps, limited our lives. But we are not only victims, which means we have the capacity to be proactive, to not only react but also consider and move in God's grace into work that God gives us. To consider—and that is the word—our world and our circumstances. To think, to think carefully, and to be in conversation with others making the best sense we can of what it means for us to respond to God, for this time and place. We want to be *intentional*.

We need resources that empower us to take personal responsibility for our own lives and our vocations. We may feel like victims living with the consequences of the decisions of others—or even our own decisions or actions, wishing we had spent more time in school or wishing we had not quit a job—but the actions of others and our own regrets need not define us. We can foster a capacity to be proactive, to name our reality but also engage that reality with confidence, hope and courage. We need not allow ourselves to be victimized by our circumstances, but can consider how God is calling us to respond with hope.

This means we choose and we act. Our vocation can be

thought of as an invitation from God in Christ. It is a calling, something to which we are beckoned, and now it is for us to respond—to choose to accept the invitation. And no one will do this for us. Each of us needs to reflect on the particulars of God's call in the midst of the particulars of our circumstances.

We can take personal responsibility for our lives. We can be stewards of the way that lies before us. We are not alone in this process of discernment and we will fulfill our vocations with others who will both help us along the way and, no doubt, stand in our way and impede us. But in the end, we are called to be stewards of our lives—our potential, our giftedness, our opportunities—and to invest our lives for the kingdom of God. We can, each one of us, look at the stage on which we have arrived and respond to the opportunity to act in response to God's call with gratitude, hope and courage.

GOOD CONVERSATION

We need to take personal responsibility for our lives and our vocation; we need to be intentional and proactive. We each will ask, *What is the good work to which I am called*? And only you or I can answer this question. We each have to make the call; no one else can do it for us. Yet it is equally important to stress that although we each make the call, we cannot do this alone. We need the company of others—co-discerners who walk with us on this road. We need fellow pilgrims who will be good conversation partners with us as we journey together on the road. At the very least, good conversation has the following qualities: it is hopeful, it is theologically informed and it is productive.

Good conversation is hopeful. Conversation about our work is easily filled with frustration. We complain about our circumstances and complain about the people we work with or the people we work for. Perhaps we complain about the situation that we face—economic or social problems that limit us. Or we feel the weight of what seem to us to be the limits that we have to live with, including the feeling that we do not get adequate support from others.

What is needed is good conversation—meaning conversation that is consistently edifying and grace-filled, that empowers us to navigate the challenges that inevitably come when we face a transition. As those who are older, do we know how to encourage and foster the capacity of those of a generation younger? As spouses, can we talk together about how we are being called, individually and together? As parents or friends, can we speak to our children and others about work that matters to us and them as fellow pilgrims trying to make sense of our lives and our work? Pastors are in conversation with their parishioners, teachers with their students, but they can only do this well if there is a resilient hopefulness that undergirds and infuses the conversation.

Good conversation is also theologically informed. By this, I mean that we have an understanding of the *meaning* of work.

We grow in our understanding of what our work means to us, to God and to the world, and we view our work through the lens of the Christian theological tradition.

Finally, good conversation is productive, meaning that it helps us see our next steps and empowers us to act. In good conversation, we enter into the wisdom that comes from the encounter with others—wisdom that provides us with headlights on a dark night.

And in all of this, we have friends, companions on the way with whom we can speak with clarity and honesty. These companions allow us to ask the hard questions, the right questions, while we know that they care about our lives, our circumstances and our challenges.

So what I am proposing here is that good conversation requires that we learn how to ask the right questions—or better put, that we learn how to *respond* to the right questions. What follows are the crucial and pivotal questions each of us needs to consider and engage:

- What on earth is God doing?
- Who are you?
- What is your stage of life?
- What are your circumstances?
- What is the cross you will have to bear?
- What are you afraid of?

There are perhaps other questions that would be pertinent to a discussion on vocation, and I will reference a couple of additional questions in the conclusion, but these six are certainly a good starting point for fruitful conversation and they provide us with a vehicle for getting to the heart of the matter. In conversation with others, we can come closer to finding clarity and courage to face what lies before us.

Focus!

In the end, good conversation about our work fosters a capacity for vocational *focus*. The six questions just mentioned actually assume a prior question, namely, *Where should I focus my time and my energy?* When we speak of focus we make an assumption: vocation is not merely about doing a good thing, but rather about doing the *right* thing. I grew up in a religious tradition where preachers were inclined to call us to "pray more, give more and serve move." Just writing this makes me shudder. "More, more, more," we were told, on the assumption that more was and is better.

Sometimes, of course, more is required. There are no doubt times when I need to be urged to pray more. And cetainly there are times when I need to be urged to serve more. But generally, most of us need a call to focus with greater intentionality. We do not need to be urged to do more. Many of us are trying to do too much! Rather, we need greater clarity about what we are truly called to and freedom to accept those things that do not need to concern us, at least in the use of our time and energy. We need to give our attention, in an age of distraction, to the zone of life and work that merits our vocational energy.

There are surely those who are underengaged, and we may think that we need to say to them, "you need to do more." There are those who are distracted or simply lazy, or those who don't really value work or appreciate the joy that comes in work. Or those who are in a malaise, living in a vocational fog, unsure what to do and with little motivation to get off the proverbial couch. But for these folks, nothing is gained by urging them to *do* more. Simply doing more is of no help to them. For all of us, the call is for greater focus.

Thus, I use the word *focus* intentionally. This may well be the crucial vocational question of our day. The capacity to focus is fundamental to manage life effectively. This has always been the case; vocational integrity has always depended on the ability to focus time and energy wisely, purposefully and courageously. But the call to focus is particularly crucial in what has been labeled an age of digital distraction. If we are going to do the right thing and do it well, it may well be that the greatest threat to that very capacity will be the propensity of our generation to be "always

> Vocation is not merely about doing a good thing, but rather about doing the *right* thing.

on," always trying to manage 101 things, including the full range of social media that we assume are essential to our lives. And the pressure to be on—always on—is vocationally insidious. It's a killer intellectually, emotionally and thus vocationally. The urgent need of our day is not so much that we would learn "time management" but rather "attention management." Where will we focus our mental, emotional and physical energy?

Now it needs to be stressed that our vocation is first and foremost to respond with gratitude to God and to grow in faith, hope and love in response to God's love and generosity toward us. But when we discern vocation, we are essentially asking a more specific question: In what particular way am I being called to respond to God? Or rather, what is the unique work that will be the expression of my faithfulness to God? That is the bottom line: responding to Christ with gratitude and trust. Discerning vocation is merely the exercise of discerning how that will find expression within the particular contours of my life.

VOCATION AND DISCERNING LOVE

Sometimes the call to pray more and give more and serve more assumes that this is the way of love. That is, the more we love God and love others, the more busy we will be. So then if you love others you will pray and give and serve, and if you love a lot you will pray and give and serve even *more*.

But this relationship between vocation and love requires greater nuance. No doubt, our calling is always a calling to love God and to love our neighbor. This is a given; vocation is always about fulfilling the call to love. Love conditions everything; it demarcates each dimension of our lives. Even when we move into solitude—the solitary work of woodworking or gardening or sermon preparation or prayer—it is still work that is done out of love for God and others.

And this is the fundamental call of the Christian: to love God and to love our neighbor. This is the baseline that informs every dimension of the work to which we are called. But do not confuse love with misguided generosity. To love well means to discern well—to discern how I am being called to love God and love others. We see this link between love and discernment in the opening chapter of the letter to the Philippians:

> And this is my prayer, that your love may overflow more
> and more with knowledge and full insight to help you
> to determine what is best, so that in the day of Christ
> you may be pure and blameless, having produced the
> harvest of righteousness that comes through Jesus Christ
> for the glory and praise of God. (Phil 1:9-11)

Love needs to be informed by knowledge and insight. We need discretion, attention and focus. Why? Because we cannot be all things to all people. And we need not. We need not even try because it is wasted energy. Rather, we need to be discerning and ask: How am I being called to fulfill the call to love in this time and place? What are the particular ways in which I am being asked to focus my time and energies as an expression of love to God and others?

VOCATION AND SABBATH

Only when we speak of focus and discernment can we begin to speak of boundaries and limits—specifically the limits of time and energy and also of sabbath. We are called to both work and rest, to work and sabbath. God rested on the seventh day and in so doing established a true rhythm for our work. Work matters, but it is only one aspect of what it means to respond to God's grace. We are not ultimately workers. We are not defined by our work. Sabbath is a fundamental practice by which we declare—in our actions—that ultimately we trust and depend on God. Sabbath is our way of indicating that we are not vindicated by our work, but rather that our work is a response to the generosity of God toward us. The pressure to pray and give and serve, more and more and more, is often a subtle way of urging us to live a lie—the lie that God responds to our work, to how much we do, and blesses us accordingly. To the contrary, our work is a response of love to the love of God, freely offered to God and to others. We are not vindicated by our work—justified before God by how much work we do or how well we do it. Rather, our work is a means by which we steward our lives in response to the grace of God freely given to us. We are doing more than we are called to do, and God is not impressed when we are overworked.

We also need to stop being impressed by those who overwork—those who neglect sabbath, the development of critical relationships or the grace of a good night's sleep. When someone claims to have not had a day off in months, we shouldn't be dazzled. Let's just say it: something is out of kilter. God would not give us so much to do that we cannot disengage from our work and observe sabbath rest. Might there be times, weeks, in which something unforeseen intrudes on sabbath? Sure. But when this becomes the norm and pattern, it is imperative that we get back to the drawing board and find a way to get at the fundamental question: What is the good work to which you are called?

PAYING ATTENTION

To answer this question requires that we learn how to be attentive. The six questions are intended to foster our capacity for attentiveness—to recognize the activity of God, the character of our world and our circumstances, and the movements of our own hearts.

In this book, I am writing on the whole for those who live active lives of intentional engagement with our world—called to business, the arts, education, religious leadership or to the good work of home making. But some readers may actually sense that they are called to what is aptly called the *contemplative* life. While my primary audience will no doubt be those who are called to be in the world, it is important that we affirm the place of those who play a vital role in the economy of God through a life of prayer, contemplation and retreat. While typically fewer in number, if this is your calling, you are an essential counterpoint to those who, like myself, are very much called to the active life. We depend on your prayers; we recognize that the routines and rhythms of your lives are vital to the tapestry of God's work in the world, and are in some ways the threads that hold that tapestry together.

What then do we mean by vocation? Well, I am using the words *vocation* and *calling* interchangeably, suggesting that by vocation we mean, quite simply, the good work to which we are called. The language of vocation assumes a predisposition in our hearts to do good work, but very specifically, we long to do the work to which our Maker invites us and for which our Maker has created us. For some, they will read what follows and think in terms of their key and core identity, seeking to flesh out the question: What is my life purpose? For most, I suspect, these questions will be pertinent as they consider the call of God for a season or chapter of life—the calling to father these children, to be the pastor of this congregation, to launch this new business venture or to establish and care for this particular garden.

As stewards of our lives attentive to the calling of God, we seek to discern our vocation and how God is inviting us to engage our world (God's world) for this time and place. To this end, we consider the potency and implications of six questions—six questions that can help us get at the big question: What is the good work to which I am called?

What on Earth Is God Doing?

Praise the LORD!
I will give thanks to the LORD with my whole heart,
   in the company of the upright, in the congregation.
Great are the works of the LORD,
   studied by all who delight in them.
Full of honor and majesty is his work,
   and his righteousness endures forever.
He has gained renown by his wonderful deeds;
   the LORD is gracious and merciful.
He provides food for those who fear him;
   he is ever mindful of his covenant.
He has shown his people the power of his works,
   in giving them the heritage of the nations.
The works of his hands are faithful and just;
   all his precepts are trustworthy.
They are established forever and ever,

to be performed with faithfulness and uprightness.
He sent redemption to his people;
    he has commanded his covenant forever.
    Holy and awesome is his name.
The fear of the LORD is the beginning of wisdom;
    all those who practice it have a good understanding.
    His praise endures forever. (Ps 111)

God is a worker. God creates, God redeems and God's work of both creation and redemption is a source of delight and encouragement. Our lives are lived in praise of God's work and in response to this work. Psalm 111:2 reads:

Great are the works of the LORD,
    studied by all who delight in them.

So this delight in the work of God helps us in considering our own work. We will come to understand our lives and our work in light of the God who is creator and redeemer of all things. This gives our lives meaning, hope and coherence. Indeed, our work—or vocation—is both an *act of response* to what God has and is doing and an *invitation from God* to be participants in this work. So we must then begin here and ask, "What on earth is God doing?" before and as part of coming to terms with what we are each called to be and to do.

As we consider this first question, I am suggesting that one of our critical needs is to develop "vocational imagination."

But this will only happen if we can grow in an appreciation of the nature and character of the work of God, as the context and foundation for our own work.

First, God is the *Creator* of all things. And this Creator God invites all to participate in this extraordinary work as co-creators: to be those who understand the created order and tend the creation and reflect the beauty of the creation through the arts. Second, God is the *Redeemer* of all things. In similar fashion, we are invited to be coworkers with God in the healing of all things (see 2 Cor 6:1). There is a sense in which all work is a participation in either the creative or the redemptive purposes of God. From this perspective, work is not a curse but an extraordinary privilege. Yes, we do need to speak of the curse when work becomes an oppressive burden, when work is nothing but toil or when meaningful and good work is not available to someone. But first we need to recognize and affirm the possibility of consciously entering into the purposes of God for and in our world.

One of the deep longings of our lives is for the gift of good work—work that matters, work that makes a difference, work that is a means by which we can express our deepest longings, aspirations and convictions. And work is good. The mission of God is not to free us from work, but to redeem us for good work. The goal of life is not less work or no work—a life of leisure—but rather a life lived engaged in the work to which we are called.

Work then is good but it is not inherently good. It is only good if it reflects the goodness of God's creation and the purposes of God in redemption. But also, work is not inherently wrong or evil. To the contrary, we have been created to do good work and will find that some of our deepest joy comes in and through the process of doing good work, work that matters to God and matters to us. And this is a powerful means by which we find meaning, integrity and coherence for our lives.

Our deep joy, when it comes to our work, is to participate in God's work. And what needs to be stressed is that God is indeed at work, as Creator and Redeemer, in every sphere and sector of our lives and our world. I grew up in a religious tradition

> The mission of God is not to free us from work, but to redeem us for good work.

that often spoke of "the Lord's work" in contrast to other forms of work or engagement. The "Lord's work" did not include business, the arts and homemaking. Rather, it was assumed that *religious* work counted and mattered and reflected the intentions and purposes of God. Secular work was not bad in itself but not the ideal to which we were called.

But could it be that God is doing good work that intersects with *every* sphere and sector of society and culture? And if so, does that mean that God is not only calling people to religious work but also to the work of business, the arts, education and indeed into the trades, the work of building and renovating homes and repairing the appliances in those homes? These each represent *good* work. Indeed, dare we say it, when a carpenter and a dentist and a farmer and a city mayor go to work they too are doing, or at least have the potential of doing, the "Lord's work" through the very work they are responsible to do that day.

DELIGHTING IN THE HANDIWORK OF GOD

All of this rests on the vision we have for the handiwork of God who is celebrated, over and over again as the Creator of all things and the Redeemer of all things. The Old Testament Psalms stress this point routinely—the God who is the maker of heaven and earth (Ps 121:2; 146:6)—affirming and delighting in the work of God, recognizing its inherent value. God is a worker, and our delight in the work of God leads us to appreciate our work as human beings.

God is the Creator. God is the Redeemer. But the witness of the book of Genesis points to something I have been indicating all along: as God's creatures, created in the image of God, we are invited to be full participants in God's work. The language of Genesis 2:5 highlights how important it is that we take our work seriously. Genesis 1 and 2 celebrate the work of the Creator who is active and engaged and delighting in this work. Again and again we read that God said it was good—indeed, at one point, we read that God said it was *very*

good. But it had yet to reach its potential; the intent of God
was not fulfilled even and specifically in what God had made.
Even though it was good, very good, something was missing.
And this brings us to Genesis 2:5:

> No plant of the field was yet in the earth and no herb
> of the field had yet sprung up—for the LORD God had
> not caused it to rain upon the earth, and there was no
> one to till the ground.

Yes, of course, until God brings the rain, the earth does not
yield its fruit. But also, there is no growth until there is the
tilling of the ground, suggesting that the human role or involvement is indispensable. The creation assumes—actually, the
Creator assumes—the active participation of the women and
men whom God will create and who will, in turn, till the earth.

So we do not merely see and observe the work of God; we
are invited to be participants in that work:

To learn how to enjoy a prairie sunset—but then also enjoy
the work of the environmental scientist.

To revel in the richness of a freshly picked apple in autumn—
and then come to an appreciation of the power of poetry to
capture that beauty in words, phrases and silences.

To watch a swallow dancing over a pond in search of food
for her young—and then hear echoes of this flight in the work
of Chopin or Debussy.

To appreciate the power of the human body—which, the

Psalmist says, is fearfully and wonderfully made—and then be in awe at the work of the surgeon who brings healing and wholeness to a broken body.

To see how God governs benevolently and with skill—and then appreciate the work of a manager or director of a non-profit agency in the heart of the city.

To see God in the person of Christ who was a master teacher—and then to recognize the art of a skilled kindergarten teacher or university professor.

In other words, our delight in the work of God is the backdrop for our appreciation of the diverse ways in which women and men are being called to participate in this work. Thus, Psalm 90:16 speaks of the work of God and is followed by this response in verse 17:

> Let the favor of the Lord our God be upon us,
>   and prosper for us the work of our hands!

There is a sense that our work is but an echo of the work of God who has created all things but who now, in Christ Jesus, is redeeming all things. In Christ, God is bringing about the fulfillment of his reign—his kingdom. And for the Christian, our work is necessarily a participation in the reign of Christ and the purposes of Christ in the world. Our vocation or calling is always "in Christ." Our lives are marked by the life, death, resurrection and ascension of Christ Jesus and the outpouring of the gift of the Spirit. So our work in the world is framed by the confidence we have that one day Christ will make all things well. This story—this narrative, the Christ narrative—shapes the contours of our lives. We do our work in response to Christ, the one through whom all things are created and are being redeemed.

THE WORK OF CO-CREATION; THE WORK OF CO-REDEMPTION

In Christ, some will be called into direct care for the created order in roles such as biologists, environmental scientists, gardeners or landscape designers. Others will be called toward a more direct involvement in the redemptive side of God's work—whether it is in religious leadership within a congregation, in evangelism, in the work of social justice or in agencies that respond to the needs of those at the margins of our society.

Most will actually do our work deeply conscious that what we are doing is in continuity with the call to Adam to till the garden and name the animals. At the same time, our work is a participation in the reign of Christ who is redeeming all things. In our work we are the hands and feet of Jesus, and whether we are bank tellers or teachers or preachers or salespersons or hospital nurses, we act and speak in the name of Christ. What I am suggesting is that just as Genesis 2 witnesses that the land does not bear its fruit until it is tilled, our work is vital to the purposes of God in the world. Our work matters.

The full beauty of the earth will not be displayed until

artists do their work. Unless there are those who partner with
God in this good work, buildings will not be built; schools
will not be established; books will not be written. As preachers
we long for women and men to know the good news, but
unless God brings the rain—again, see Genesis 2:5—it will
not happen. In like fashion, as preachers we have to do the
"tilling" to which we are called, without which the purposes
of God will not be fulfilled in the lives of those to whom we
are called to preach.

Thus our work as preachers, artists, business men and
women, educators, designers and police officers is vital and
essential and it matters. We do our work because it matters.
And we do it in the name of Christ.

All work that is done in the name of Christ must take account of the commitment of God to economic and social
justice. God's call on our lives will always be one in which we
are invited to enter into the longing of God for justice and
peace. And so we do not do our work—whether in business
or school or in any calling—in a way that enriches ourselves
at the expense of others. Rather, our work must necessarily
always be a participation in the commitment to be agents of
God's restorative justice.

When this is our perspective—that we are living and acting
and speaking in the name of Christ as his agents—we are
drawn more closely to Christ in our work. In other words,
our work becomes an actual means by which we grow in faith,

hope and love; our work becomes an integral part of our spiritual journey. And along the way we will occasionally have these extraordinary moments or seasons when we have a keen sense that we are the hands and feet of Christ and that when we speak, we speak for God. We do not presume, of course; our motives and our work will never be purely one and the same as what God is doing.

What we learn in all of this is that God is calling women and men into every sphere and sector of society, and that the church makes a difference when it empowers its members to be God's people in the community and in the world. What would it mean for the church to be a garden of vocations where we recognize that the most significant thing about a church is not its size, but its capacity to empower women and men to be agents for Christ Monday through Friday in the businesses, homes, schools, art galleries, civic offices and taxis of our cities? What would it look like for the Sunday morning preaching to empower and equip people for the work to which they are headed that week, whether it is driving a taxi or launching a new entrepreneurial enterprise, whether caring for young children at home or teaching at the local university?

May you have the joy of speaking at a gathering when you sense an uncanny alignment with the Spirit. May you know the joy of working in a garden; as you plant a tree may you be aware of the alignment of the stars in that moment and sense the very handiwork of God. And may you know the pleasure of God as you raise a child, manage a bank or fly an airplane with a precious cargo of passengers. May you know, in significant measure, that what you are doing is the *Lord's work*. And may you know this joy even in the ordinary, everyday activities of the work to which you have been called.

FOSTERING A FULL APPRECIATION OF THE WORK OF GOD

Surely one of the primary tasks of the church is the affirmation of the diverse ways in which God is calling women and men to speak and to act in the world in the name of Christ. Sunday morning sermons would then be week in and week out reminders of the grand purposes of God in the world. Sermons would not only address morality [how to be a better Dad], but rather draw us into the remarkable narrative of creation, fall and redemption, to see and appreciate the reign of Christ and be reminded weekly that our work matters because it matters to God and is part of what God is doing in our world. Each person can, in some modest way, see their work as an invitation into the mission of God.

So why not have a brief ceremony at the end of the academic year when all who have graduated as engineers or accountants or school teachers are prayed for as they enter into the work place? Why not highlight how many nurses there are in the congregation and pray that God would empower them to be salt and light in the hospital? Why not ask all the taxi drivers to stand and bless them as they fan out across the city with the capacity to speak words of grace and peace again and again through the day? This ceremony would celebrate the first-grade teacher as much as the university professor, the bank manager as much as those who are being called to oversee the homeless shelter, seeing all as part of the wonderful tapestry of God's work in the world.

Several years ago I had the privilege to visit the Hanoi Christian Fellowship, which is an international congregation that meets weekly on Sunday morning in a hotel ballroom in the Vietnamese capital. I had served previously as senior pastor of an international congregation so I was naturally interested in this congregation and was struck—deeply impressed—by the phenomenal variety of people who had gathered for worship. It seemed from the dress and accents from all over the world that for the majority, worshiping in English was not their first language but the language that brought them together.

After the morning worship service, I asked around, eager to know what brought all of these expatriates to Hanoi, Vietnam. When I caught up to one of the leaders of the congregation, I got a response. "Well, I would estimate," he said, "that about a third of those present are directly involved in kingdom-related ministries." "Oh," I said, "and what about the rest—what brings them to Hanoi?" And he gave me the expected response: that many are in diplomatic service, this being the capital city, others are involved in business and then others are involved in education, teaching in the University of Hanoi and other institutions of higher education.

I was stunned by this response. The implication, however subtle, was that those in diplomatic, business and educational interests were not in "kingdom-related" ministries, by which I suspect he meant those who were in community development or some kind of religious work.

We urgently need churches, in the West and the East, North and South, that embrace a vision for all the ways in which God is at work—in our cities, towns and villages—calling women and men to participate in "the Lord's work" of bringing about his kingdom purposes for our world in our time.

> In our worship we empower God's people to be players in the work of God in the world.

In our worship, we delight in the work of God as Creator and Redeemer. And in that same worship we empower God's people to be players in the work of God in the world. Our sermons and hymns and prayers are not escapist; rather, they very intentionally respond to the world in which business people, artists and educators actually live and work and then, with equal intentionality, speak to, empower and encourage those who are called into the shops, schools and studios from Monday through Friday.

FOSTERING A VOCATIONAL IMAGINATION

What all of this suggests to me is that one of our great challenges is to foster what we might call a "vocational imagination" in our preaching, in how we illustrate our sermons or in the way that we profile the diverse ways in which people are called into service for God and for the kingdom of God. In our homes and in our churches we need to foster a theological literacy, a grand vision for the purposes of God in the world.

Surely this fostering of a vocational imagination begins at home. One of the most powerful gifts we give our children is to expose them to all the diverse ways in which women and men participate in the work of God. We can take them on visits to carpenter shops, artist studios, small businesses and factories, or provide opportunity to see scholars at work in libraries, pastors attending to the concerns of a congregation and chefs in the kitchen of a busy restaurant. As parents we should delight in each and assure our children that they would be affirmed and celebrated in whatever line of work to which they are called. We make our homes places of a wide and gracious vocational imagination, celebrating all the possible ways our children might be called of God.

Some homes, unfortunately, have a very narrow vocational imagination. It is so easy for parents to lionize one vocation over another. In my growing up, my world tended to profile the missionary who went to another culture and country. The assumption was that the only good outcome for children was religious work. But I know others who grew up with a father and grandfather who were medical doctors, so those friends lived with the continual expectation that John III would also follow in their footsteps, and that all their children would enter into the "professions." They were not exposed to or encouraged to consider other possibilities, to see what it is that captures their imaginations.

We all long for significance, and one of the most powerful sources of that longing arises from our family or origin. We long to be significant in the eyes of our parents, our community and our society. And each culture and each subculture has a script: if you follow this script, then you will be a significant person.

Ask yourself: What is the script that was promoted, explicitly or subtly by my parents, by the preachers on Sunday or by my religious subculture? What was that vision of human success? And then, as God grants you grace, step back and consider, weigh carefully. Take full account of your home and upbringing and get a good read on what your culture affirms and honors as worthwhile and significant professions.

If you sense that God's purpose in this world is more all-encompassing, then have the courage to go against the grain, taking in the full scope of God's own work as Creator and Redeemer of all things. Crucial in this regard is that our vocational imagination take account of God's commitment and priority to justice. What is it about the work of God in the world that captures your imagination, that stirs your heart and beckons for participation?

So what on earth is God doing? What all of this means is that our story—our personal story, the journey of our life and work—is informed by and shaped by and given meaning by another story, namely, the God-story. The narrative that makes sense of it all is the story of God as Creator and Redeemer. In our worship we come back to this story again and again—the story of God who in Christ is bringing about the peace of all things and making all things new.

Who Are You?

O LORD, you have searched me and known me.
You know when I sit down and when I rise up;
    you discern my thoughts from far away.
You search out my path and my lying down,
    and are acquainted with all my ways.
Even before a word is on my tongue,
    O LORD, you know it completely.
You hem me in, behind and before,
    and lay your hand upon me.
Such knowledge is too wonderful for me;
    it is so high that I cannot attain it. (Ps 139:1-6)

Later in the same Psalm we come to these amazing words:

For it was you who formed my inward parts;
    you knit me together in my mother's womb.
I praise you, for I am fearfully and wonderfully made.

Wonderful are your works;
that I know very well. (Ps 139:13-14)

Vocational discernment is never just about discerning or getting excited about what God is doing in the world. I can get quite enthused about the work of business and celebrate those who are called into the production of goods and services. I often imagine that I could do a good job in business and be an entrepreneur.

I am also quite taken with the work of artists, whether as painters, landscape designers or musicians. And there are days I can imagine myself a musician or an artist. I can hear the Vancouver Symphony Orchestra perform Beethoven's Ninth and conclude as I return to the parking lot that I have found my calling: conducting symphony orchestras!

Both when I was a high school student and a university student, my favorite professors were all in the history department and I consistently enjoyed those courses the most. In my early twenties, I often thought I could very well at some point see myself as a history professor—perhaps in a high school, or even in a university. I was fascinated by history, enjoyed experiencing it well taught and easily imagined myself in a similar role.

We can consider what God is doing that might be catching our attention, and we might be moved by many possibilities. But then we also need to ask the second question: Who am I? Or, much like the urging of the Apostle Paul to the Romans, we each need to take a considered, patient and honest look at ourselves (Rom 12:3).

THE WISDOM OF KNOWING GOD AND KNOWING SELF

Sober self-reflection is an essential counterpart to our delight in the work of God. We might easily be inspired by what others are doing for and with God. But self-knowledge is critical to the process of vocational discernment.

Frankly, I get a little nervous when a college chapel service has an inspirational speaker who might persuade us all to become social workers or medics, or whatever that individual does. We need to slow down and ask the hard question: Yes, but who am *I*? We need role models. We need those who might inspire us to significant possibilities. Of course we need to be encouraged to take on something bigger than ourselves. But take it slowly.

In my religious context we often speak of the presence of a guest speaker who comes from a distant land, perhaps as a missionary, inspires us with what God is doing there and then concludes the presentation with an invitation to young people to give their lives in foreign service. And young, impressionable teens, eager to please their own community—knowing that if they respond they will get affirmation—can easily choose to respond without doing the necessary, essential and basic work of sober self-reflection.

Can a fifteen-year-old receive a call to work with refugees

while hearing an inspirational talk? Certainly. Of course this is possible. Is it *likely*? Not really. This is not God's normal way of issuing calls. Should we try for it? When nothing is really gained by pressing for an early commitment, why would we?

Further, however inspirational the talk, there is no substitute for a solid, clear-minded, sober look at ourselves. And this takes time. Most teens do not know themselves well enough to respond to a call. For most it will come later as they move into adulthood, as I will stress when we come to question three.

The "who am I" question rests on a profound theological principle: God's call on our lives is consistent with who God made us to be. If the first question we must ask is about how God is at work in the world, the second question must be about ourselves. We can only discern

> God's call on our lives is consistent with who God made us to be.

vocation well if we have a maturing self-knowledge. And, as I will stress, it is not about who we *wish* we were, but who we *actually* are. Vocational discernment is about seeing ourselves in truth and accepting and embracing who we are. It is about coming to the grace of not wishing we were anyone other than who we are: to see ourselves as created by God, with this range of strengths, capacities, desires and opportunities. Vocational discernment is ultimately about the stewardship of our lives.

The sequence is important. We begin with God's story of the creation of the world and then also the work of Christ, the cosmic Lord. Our significance is located in our lives within the narrative of God's purposes in the world. But then we ask the next question: How is God inviting me to be part of this story? We appreciate that we matter to God; we recognize the significance of our human identity. We are, in the words of the psalmist, "fearfully and wonderfully made." The psalmist surely celebrates the work of God. But what also strikes us is that this is complemented by the celebration of our human identity and potential.

We can rightly affirm our human identity and ask, Who am I, and how am I—as I have been designed and created to be a means by which God is glorified—being called into God's purposes for the world?

As already noted, this question assumes that God's call on our lives is not arbitrary. There are no generic people. Rather in the wisdom of God and the providential care of God for God's world, we can affirm that there is a stunning diversity to the human race, and that every day we meet people who see the world differently and respond differently according to how God has wired them. Deep in their DNA—their psyche, in the deepest recesses of their hearts—is a way of seeing and responding and acting that is, very simply, who they are.

I am not suggesting that we are naive to the destructive power of sin in our lives. Of course not. We are so easily caught up in a self-centered cycle of pride, selfishness, envy and greed. And yet, surely part of our faith journey is to peel back the darkness that so easily infects our lives and seek the grace of God to know ourselves in truth. This truly is the way of humility: to stop wishing we were anyone other than who we are, and ask the hard and honest questions—liberating questions, actually—regarding our true identity. We no longer need to live by pretense, carrying on with a mask or a persona that is, in the end, a weight, like clothing that does not fit us.

THE CHALLENGE OF TRULY KNOWING OURSELVES

Now, a mature self-knowledge is not something we come by easily. There are so many pressure points, from parents, teachers and even friends and our own desire to be accepted and liked and affirmed. It can be so difficult to peel back the layers of pretense and get to the heart of our identity, to the deep sense of who we are. But we must, because wisdom is found here. The wise are always those who know God and know the ways of God. But the wise are also those who come to the gracious and liberating truth of their own self-identity.

Parents play a vital role in this process by empowering each child to be at peace with themselves, affirming their individuality, their likes and dislikes, their proclivities, watching and affirming with delight how each child finds genuine self-expression. Teachers of every grade also play a vital role. I think here of the influence of my grade twelve history teacher,

Henry Veltmeyer, who so affirmed the individual identities of his students and seemed to actually revel in our diverse ways of being and seeing and responding to him and to his class.

Through the early adult years, we can begin to encourage diversity of experience and opportunity. Giving young adults the freedom to fail allows them to explore different avenues of engagement with their world. I think of the young man who spent a year in engineering studies with the full support of his parents and who then, after a year recognized (still with the full support of parents and friends) that "engineering is not me." That time of testing those waters was merely part of the process of self-discovery. No harm done.

GETTING TO THE HEART OF THE MATTER

Along the way we ask questions: Who am I? What captures my imagination? What bothers me most? Where do I have interests and aptitudes? And yet increasingly I find that the rather simple yet profound question, "What is it that matters to you and matters perhaps more than anything?" is a helpful way to get to the heart of the matter. Not always, of course. Sometimes what matters to us is a resolution to a pressing problem, or perhaps we are sitting in a hospital and the only thing that matters to us is the health of our child. But when we have some distance from pressing concerns, and ask what it might mean if we only have one life to live—which just happens to be the case—and when immediate crises and concerns are set aside for the time being, what is it about ourselves that emerges on the table before us?

There is no doubt that for me, my move into administration arose very clearly out of a deep concern for the importance and potential of education—in my case, higher education in particular—to be a means by which society, the church and individuals' lives are shaped and transformed. I believe in it; it *matters* to me.

I have a friend who is deeply convinced that through business—the production of goods and services—he can make a substantive difference, and that this matters. It matters enough to him to go at it each week, through joys and sorrows, ups and downs.

I think of the lawyer for whom the legal system matters, who believes that honoring that system is the only way a society can exist in peace. The artist, for whom the place of beauty is not something secondary to life but essential—so essential that life is hardly worth living without it.

Then there is the woman who has been teaching kindergarten children for thirty years with the deep conviction that this age group matters and that these tender shoots need to be tended to with grace, humor, love and wisdom.

I am also reminded of the mayor who recognizes that her work can be a major factor in the livability and civility of the city that has elected her to office.

And then I have my visits to the dentist, who with remarkable patience stresses again the need to floss because, well, it matters. The condition of my teeth matters to her! And I'm glad that my teeth matter to her, however strange that sounds.

I know an executive assistant for whom the smooth and effective functioning of the vice president's office matters. And I value the basketball coach, for whom the capacity of his team to maximize their potential matters enough to work patiently and persistently with each player and with the team as a whole to bring out their very best.

Again I stress that the sequence by which we come to this question is important: we only ask the question, "What matters to me?" after we have learned to consider what it is that matters to God. We need to devote our energies to that which truly matters, so we anchor our reflections in the prior question—what is it that matters to God. But then, given the full scope of what God is doing in the world, we test our own hearts.

FROM WHAT MATTERS TO THE QUESTION OF CAPACITY

Now I am not suggesting that it is *only* a question of what matters to you. Many things matter to me that do not reflect my particular calling: I long for peace between Israel and Palestine, but for now at least I am not being called to play a direct role in that conflict. I long for the city in which I live to have an excellent public transportation system, but I am not—at least for now—being called to lay down tracks for light rail transit. And yet, the question of what matters is still a good place to begin in the process of self-knowledge.

Having asked the prior question—what it is that matters to you—then, and perhaps only then, we need to ask the capacity question. You may care very much about quality preaching but not have the God-given ability to preach well. You may say that quality financial accounting matters a great deal. Most assuredly it does; it should matter to all of us. But accountants typically are those for whom "what matters" is matched by a capacity with numbers and accounts and financial systems. Capacity is essential, and yet, perhaps what we need to stress is that ability or capacity follows conviction about what matters.

If good administration matters to you, then develop the capacity—the craft—to do it well. If the arts matter, you may well have an innate gift for drawing or music or theater, but that gift will need to be honed and cultivated. And what sustains you through the development of the craft, to master the craft—of teaching or administration or music or writing or accounting—is that this work matters and it matters to you. Skill development and the cultivation of our capacity for something are a response to vocation. Giftedness does not, ultimately, determine vocation but is rather in the service of vocation.

Part of this process of vocational discernment is to come to a gracious acceptance not only of the capacity and skills that need to be honed and developed, but also of our limitations.

And rather than bemoaning the limits, we should learn to live within them and learn what it means in the exercise of our own abilities to lean into and depend on the abilities and capacities of others.

What I am saying is that God's call on our lives will fit reasonably—and I use the word *reasonably* intentionally—within a considered assessment of who we are. Vocation is not found through some great spark of light, not typically, at least. We will not likely have an angel come and visit us as Mary did. Rather, for most of us it will come through the diligence of asking questions, thinking clearly and carefully, weighing possibilities and coming to what is, as my colleague at Ambrose University, Jonathan Goosen, has put it, a "rationally satisfying" way of seeing ourselves.

Jonathan pointed out to me that he "grew up thinking that God's call must always be the unexpected, the dissonant, that which confounded reason; that these qualities were marks of the rightly spiritual" sense of call. While he acknowledges that such a calling is surely possible, it is not the norm. For most of us our calling will, quite simply, make sense; it will fit us like a tailor-made piece of clothing.

Now some may protest that this focus on the self and on self-knowledge seems to run contrary to the call to give up our lives for the sake of Christ and live in generous and even sacrificial service for others. In response I suggest that "for Christ" and "for others" is indeed our fundamental reference point.

But we still ask: How can I be a steward of this life, and how has God uniquely cultivated in my heart a vision for what matters and the capacity to do something about it? What is the best way I can live my life for Christ and for others in a way that is consistent with how God has created me? Self-knowledge is not, then, an act of selfishness or self-centeredness, but an act of stewardship, of seeing ourselves in truth so that we can live in truth for Christ and for others.

> What is the best way I can live my life for Christ and for others in a way that is consistent with how God has created me?

However, we do need to be alert to how the focus on self can easily lead to self-absorption. There are four key means by which we counter this propensity in our hearts.

First, we always *prioritize question number one—What on earth is God doing?* As I have stressed, our lives are located in the big picture. We are participants in the grand narrative, the work of the Creator and Redeemer. It is not, in the end, all about what we are up to, but rather what God is up to.

Second, we *recognize our capacity for self-deception and self-rationalizations.* We can so easily be taken with roles and responsibilities that seem adventurous or grand, or we can be captured by the allure of either fame or fortune. The pressure points within our family systems can be just as powerful, so we want to be aware of ways we might be overly susceptible to the desires to please family.

Third, we *consistently come back to the law of love.* We need to take a sober look at ourselves with the end always in mind that we can more effectively respond to the call to love our neighbor as ourselves and to serve others generously.

And fourth, we *see that self-knowledge is always a matter of graciously accepting, in humility, our limits as much as our strengths.* In this way we learn what it means to lean into and depend on the capacities of others. Ironically, an inordinate focus on the self can, indeed, distort our capacity to see ourselves in truth. But we seek to always know ourselves as those with whom we are in community know us. We seek to truly know and be truly known by those called to participate in the purposes in the world.

The Christian community, including the ministry of preaching, can play a vital role. The church and the Sunday sermon can be part of how God graciously empowers individuals to know the grace of humility and self-knowledge. And nothing is more crucial here than the love of Christ. Nothing. We will not know ourselves and accept ourselves—embrace our identity—unless we know that we are loved and accepted by Christ.

In this regard, few things are more powerful than parents who love their children uniquely—refusing to compare them to one another and allowing each to be distinct, to be wired differently, and affirming and delighting in these differences. And the church can be a community that echoes the life in the home with an intentional affirmation of the diversity of people who are present for and with the congregation each Sunday, including all the many ways in which God is calling our children and our young people into service for the kingdom. But young people will not be freed to see themselves in truth unless they know the love and acceptance of the Christian community.

Preachers play a pivotal role here: First, as we discussed in question number one, by affirming the whole scope of the purposes of God in the world. But then also by affirming the diversity of people who make up a congregation and preaching the Scriptures in such a way that hearers are empowered toward living in humility—the gracious humility of not wishing they were anyone other than who they are.

REFLECTION, AWARENESS AND ACCEPTANCE

As we think on this important question of who we are, there are three more things to keep in mind. First, one of the most valuable means by which we foster self-knowledge is through an intentional reflection on experience—on past successes, failures, joys and sorrows. A journal is a potentially helpful tool for monitoring the movement of our hearts and attending to the emotional contours of our lives, the traces that are left by our various work experiences. And, taken together, we tend to see that there is a thread through it all that is, for many, a profound revelation, a self-disclosure that is a critical means of knowing of our true selves.

Second, remember that if you do not take the lead on this and reflect who you are, there are many out there more than happy to tell you who you should be and what you should be like. If we are passive on this matter, we lose. We have to be intentional and determined; we cut against the grain, forging our identity and clarifying our vocation in the face of those who have an agenda for us.

Third, what all of this speaks to is a maturing self-awareness which necessarily includes a growing self-acceptance. We stop wishing we are anyone other than who we are. Increasingly I see that this mature self-awareness and acceptance presumes something so very fundamental: we know that God knows us, loves us and accepts us.

So we choose to give thanks for this life and in so doing, we choose to then offer it back to God as a gift, to God and to others.

What Is Your Life Stage?

Give ear, O my people, to my teaching;
    incline your ears to the words of my mouth.
I will open my mouth in a parable;
    I will utter dark sayings from of old,
things that we have heard and known,
    that our ancestors have told us.
We will not hide them from their children;
    we will tell to the coming generation
the glorious deeds of the LORD, and his might,
    and the wonders that he has done.

He established a decree in Jacob,
    and appointed a law in Israel,
which he commanded our ancestors
    to teach to their children;
that the next generation might know them,

the children yet unborn,
and rise up and tell them to their children,
so that they should set their hope in God,
and not forget the works of God,
but keep his commandments. (Ps 78:1-7)

The journey of life is remarkably simple, in a way: we are born, we live a short span of perhaps four score years and then we die. We cross over to the other side. This is the journey of life, the pilgrimage from birth to death.

Psalm 78, like many other Psalms, speaks of the transmission of life, wisdom and faith from one generation to the next. We look back to our ancestors, and we look ahead to those as yet unborn. Wisdom is passed down from one generation to the next—like the baton in a race. And the question is whether we will carry that baton with grace, generosity and courage. The Psalmist essentially asks if we will be a generation that gets this: Will we, in our time, be faithful to God as we pass on the faith of our ancestors to our children and through them to those as yet unborn?

To answer the vocation question—What is God's call on my life?—we have to ask, "What on earth is God doing?" And then we need to ask the personal question, "Who am I?" But we also need to locate our reflections on vocation within this extraordinary journey, this process, as we move through the seasons of life. We locate ourselves intergenerationally, considering our calling from the vantage point of the journey of an adult life. Vocational discernment looks and feels very different depending where we are on this road. And while there are a whole host of variables that inform and influence our discernment throughout our adult lives, many have found it helpful to think in terms of three distinct and critical transition points in the life of an adult:

- The move from adolescence into early adulthood

- The move into our mid-adult years, which for many will be from our mid-thirties till sometime in our sixties

- The move into our senior years

Each of these is a necessary transition, a signpost along our way, marking the transitions of life as we grow up, grow older and eventually cross over. There will be gains and losses, even necessary losses, that are all part of growing up, embracing life and then letting go of one stage so we can move on and embrace the next. And we only live well when we see this, when we not merely accept that this is life, but engage life to the full through those transitions, through those gains and losses.

For young adults, the big question is, Will you assume adult responsibility for your life?

For mid-adults, increasingly the question is one of focus: Will you focus your time, energy and money on that which truly matters to you?

And for those of us who are moving into our senior years,

will we begin to shift our energy and let go of the levers of power and empower the next generation, passing on blessings, wisdom and encouragement?

You might be tempted, as you read what follows, to jump to your own life stage and skip the other two—perhaps thinking that as a twenty-something you don't need to think about the later stages of an adult life, or that as an older person the earlier stages are no longer pertinent.

And yet we need to be regularly reminded that we are often in conversation with others—family, friends, colleagues—who may well be at another stage of life and work, so it only makes sense that in conversation with them we have some sense of the unique challenges or issues they are facing. More than that, what needs to be stressed is that this is all part of a single journey from birth to life, even if there are different phases or stages along the road.

THE EARLY ADULT YEARS

The move into adulthood—likely in one's twenties—is a great opportunity for self-discovery, exploration, testing and trying different possibilities. There will be some child prodigies that by age ten already know they will be concert pianists or the fifteen-year-old who is already in line to become a professional soccer player. But those are the exceptions. Most young people do not know themselves well enough to discern their vocations in any final or definite sense; they have not lived with themselves long enough to know what it is that matters to them. Thus the early adult years are an opportunity to get to know themselves in the context of personal growth, learning and opportunities for work.

Perhaps you take courses in your college years that reflect an emerging interest for you. And yet, I often stress for undergrads, keep your options open as long as possible. Take electives that open up areas of potential interest—a course in geology if you are a history major or a course in art history if you are a science major.

A part-time job as a college student might also be as significant as a science course for fostering self-knowledge and vocational discernment. Some choose to take what is often called a "gap year" after high school graduation. This can be perhaps a year to work: planting trees in the far north, apprenticing to a trade, or immersed as a volunteer in a local church. Or if finances allow, it could be a year of travel: a form of exploration and learning and discovery, but of a different sort than formal studies in a community college or university. In my own case, I took a year for travel between my third and fourth years of my undergraduate studies and have no doubt that that year was as formative as any in my transition into adulthood.

Yet through these years—typically our early twenties—the defining issue is captured by a word introduced into our lexicon by adult developmental theorists: *differentiation*. The early adult years are first and foremost years in which we move from being children who belong to our parents into adulthood where we learn what that means and embrace the opportunity to take adult responsibility for our own lives.

This does not mean that we necessarily dismiss our parents or dishonor them. Of course not. And some have protested the use of the word *differentiation* precisely because they suggest that it frames these years too much in terms of the parents. So maybe we state it differently and instead speak of it as the years when we learn to take adult responsibility for our own lives. All good of course, except for the crucial issue at hand: If we take adult responsibility for our lives, are we willing to assume a role that until now has been the role of our parents?

So differentiation does not mean that we dismiss—or even less, dishonor—our parents. But it does require an appreciation of the ultimate priority: to know ourselves before God, to qualify the role of our parents and locate our relationship with them in its proper perspective. We appreciate their input, but as adults we learn to find our own way before God and in response to our own identity.

For most young people, some kind of distance—social and geographic distance—is needed. Perhaps some are off to a distant country to volunteer in an orphanage or away at college or university, not down the street but actually far enough away that coming home on the weekends is simply not always convenient. The distance may well be crucial for most, offering social and geographic space so that we gradually come to an awareness of our own identity. To make decisions—daily decisions about food and accommodation and time management—but also enter into a range of social interactions that are not mediated by our parents. This is crucial, essential to our vocational development.

As the president of a university I celebrate those parents who are highly invested in their sons and daughters, so invested that they are at the opening of the academic year dropping off their children, lugging gear for them into their residences and helping them get the lay of the land. But then, I say, "Okay . . . all good. Now leave them and give them time and space. Lots of it." Their social, intellectual, emotional, spiritual and vocational development requires parents who are not brooding over them or checking in continually or fretting about them. What these students need most is an opportunity to find themselves, and this requires time and space. So I say to their parents, "Go home." It needs to be said calmly and gently, but it needs to be said. "Go home and allow your daughter or your son to begin the necessary next steps of finding themselves and, sooner than later, take adult responsibility for their own lives."

And in these critical, liminal years, one of the most vital roles will be played by other adults—be they employers, teachers, coaches or older men and women in the congregation where these young people worship—who come along as an alternate voice to their parents. These other adults can bless our young adults, listen and counsel and help mediate the process of coming into adult responsibility. Young people *need* older adults—people who are the same generation as their parents but aren't their parents—who celebrate their identity, believe in them, bless them and encourage them.

Women and men need an environment shaped by older adults that is both secure and empowering: a safe place to explore possibilities and get some distance from parental expectations. These emerging adults need some freedom from gender stereotypes (cultural assumptions regarding typical female or male occupations) as they come to a sense of self. In time this means a profound degree of self-acceptance, though this might not come until they are over forty. But it can come and it must come in relationships and friendships that strengthen their capacity for self-acceptance. A knowledge of self and a valuing of self emerges, making them ready to engage the world on their own terms, as individuals with their own voice.

So when we speak of differentiation we do not mean radical individualism. Rather, we learn to move into community and interdependence. But the key reality is that we live before God, in community, on our own terms; our relationship with God and with our community is no longer mediated for us by our parents.

THE MID-ADULT YEARS

The mid-adult years are those years in which the word *focus* becomes more relevant and pertinent than perhaps any time in our lives. We may have struggled with focus as a young person, and understandably so since it seemed there were so many possibilities, so many things that interested us, so many options for doing good things. And that is perhaps as it should be. But moving into our middle adult years, it is imperative that we begin to get a sense of "if this is who I am, then I need to begin to act on this." As I suggested earlier, the question of focus is always going to be important. And yet, at no time is it more important or more crucial than in our mid-adult years. As young people we may not know where we should focus our time, energy and attention. And in our senior years we have limited energy and no choice but to focus. But in our mid-adult years, so much seems possible. We have boundless energy and feel we can take on so many things, willing (and able) to put in long hours. And so easily we take on this, that and the other, and live (and try to work) perpetually distracted by all that seemingly demands our attention.

Focus is crucial and now is the time to learn the art, for if we do not learn how to focus now, it is fair to ask if we ever will. Once we reach our mid-thirties, or, at the very least by our early forties, we need clarity. And that clarity—the emerging focus—is shaped by a two-part self-awareness.

First, we have now lived with ourselves long enough to

have a sense of our innate abilities. Some will have this clearly in hand when they are younger. But for most, this awareness will emerge later. There is a sense in which we could not have this kind of focus in our lives because we did not know ourselves well enough until now to come to this kind of focus. For most, it will not be until their thirties that they really know what it is that they are good at, or better put, have the *potential* to be good at.

Note that distinction: you are not yet a master. But is there the innate ability, the capacity, that only lacks training, practice, coaching and mentoring?

This decision to focus time and energy often requires great courage, especially for those who have been pursuing occupations for reasons that now seem not quite right: seeking financial security, pleasing one's parents or a misguided pursuit of some kind of prestige. Just as it was a huge act of courage for the young person to seek distance from parents, this is equally an act of courage. Why? Because saying yes to one thing means saying no to 101 other possibilities. Now we begin to see that we cannot be everything we might want to be, so we drill down, make the move, focus our energies, recognize what it is that matters to us and manage our time and priorities accordingly.

It means that we recognize where we have God-given abilities and talents to make a difference, but it also means we learn to face our *limitations,* to graciously accept what we are perhaps not so good at. And we come to view this not as a problem but actually as a kind of gift; it helps us focus and recognize where our time and energy should be invested.

Here is where we need to be astute about not assuming too much from what has been a focus for us so far in our lives. For example, I was struck by the courage of a young man—thirty-nine years of age—who at a seminar I led on vocation acknowledged to others that he was trained in medicine and had a family practice but that this was simply not his calling. It was good work and it paid well, but it was not the work to which he was called. His grandfather had been a doctor, his father was a doctor and there was huge family pressure for him to follow in their footsteps. But the seminar had given him the language to say the words: "This is not me." And what was powerful was that his formal education was not going to be the determining factor in his vocational discernment. Was his education wasted? Of course not. But neither can it be viewed as an obligation. At most, our formal studies are only one factor in vocational discernment.

Or I think of the young man who was clearly a gifted and capable auto salesman, so much so that at a very young age he had become the sales manager of the local dealership. And here too, he was earning well and had what might easily be thought of as a secure job and a clear career path ahead of him. But there was a nagging in his spirit, something that he had to face: he was not at ease with the culture of the business, he was not doing what he most wanted to do, not to mention that he had an increased desire to be his own boss. So he walked away from it. And while he struggled at first to find his way in his own business, he did not doubt it was the right thing for him. He has not looked back. Was his experience as

> Letting go of idealism does not mean we let go of dreams and ambition.

a sales manager wasted? No, not at all. But it was, at most, only one factor in this man's vocational discernment process.

There is a gracious movement from idealism—thinking we can be anything and will be heroes fixing the world's problems—to a naming of the actual life that is before us. By letting go of idealism I do not mean we let go of dreams and ambition. Not at all. But now, these dreams—the aspiration of our hearts—fit who we are and fit our world, our context, our lives. Now our sense of purpose fits us and we begin to invest time and energy to live out of that reality.

As noted, this will require courage. Saying yes to our lives will mean saying no to that which is not us. But if we manage this transition—essentially a spiritual crisis—with wisdom and grace, it will be one of the most significant growth points of our lives. It requires a profound level of honesty—we stop living with illusions about who we are or wish we were—and accept the life that has been given to us. We embrace it, we choose it, we walk with it.

The evidence that we have made this move, this transition, is our *focus*, our resolve—not every day but on many a day—to do what we must do, to prioritize our time and our energy. If you are a poet, it means finding the time to put down at the very least a few lines. If you are a preacher, it means that you will devote the necessary time that it takes to come to Sunday morning with the right word in season. For the entrepreneur, you wade in the deep end and do what it takes to get your new business off the ground. It means turning off the cell phone, ignoring the email inbox and giving attention to that which is important not merely urgent.

If we are going to thrive vocationally in our mid-adult years, focus is imperative. Foundational. But there are two other things that are very close seconds, almost as critical as focus in our vocational development.

First, we have to master our craft. It is now or never. Well, okay, maybe that is an overstatement. But if so, barely so. Now it is the time to drill down and pursue the way of excellence. For example, I think of the young faculty member at a university: mid-thirties, doctoral studies completed, now in a position where she has the possibility to grow and develop professionally. Bear down, I say, and learn the craft to which you are called: master the art of teaching and classroom instruction; get about your research and writing and learn to do it well. Learn, early on, how to be a participant—a good and winsome player—in faculty governance and contribute in a way that fosters institutional vitality.

Or the preacher, now in his thirties, who works diligently and persistently on preaching—exegesis, sermon construction, delivery—knowing that he will not have mastered the craft until he has preached three or four hundred sermons. He does not mind being the pastor of a smaller congregation because it frees him from some of the pressures that inevitably face larger congregations, offering him the time and space to develop his craft. And he hones it, welcoming critique and response and comments from parishioners and others, not defensively, but taking each bit of insight anyone will give. He wants to do what he is called to do and do it very well.

Second, few things are more crucial to this stage of our vocational development than learning how to work with others. We come to this through a recognition of our need for others and our appreciation for their abilities and contributions. A writer realizes that she needs an editor, they both appreciate that neither of them has the skills of a publisher, and everyone knows that there are marketers and booksellers and librarians that make their contribution to the process of getting a written work into the hands of a reader. Artists need to cooperate with galleries so their work comes before potential buyers. Academics recognize their need for keen and capable accountants and finance officers to manage institutional funds. No one fulfills their vocation alone but only in interdependency upon others. We thrive vocationally in the mid-adult years when we grow in our capacity to work with others, lean on the abilities and talents of others, value their competency and wisdom and together accomplish something that reflects the synergy of talent and commitment.

What do mid-adults need from their families, their friends and their church community? They need *acceptance*: people who embrace them and love them as they are. They need *encouragement*: words of truth from those who know them and recognize the courage required to persevere. And they need *accountability*: honest questions that foster their capacity to live their lives.

Remember this: in your mid-adult years, you are taking responsibility for *your* life. No one else will do it for you. Don't expect the company or organization you work for to manage your life. It is yours to be lived in response to the call of God. And yet, as I will stress in the conclusion to this book, you cannot do this alone. In midlife you still need to find the blessing of those who have gone before you and you assuredly need the company of friends.

SENIOR ADULT YEARS

And then we come to our senior years. The timing of this transition will vary, of course, but typically we move into our senior years sometime in our sixties. This is as critical a transition as either the move into early adulthood or into our mid-adult years. And if those who argue that our seventies may be some of the most fruitful and productive years of our lives are right, then this move may be the most critical of all. Now we become the sages—the wise women and men, the elders within the community—leveraging our lives and our vocations for the well-being of others and our world. And we have the potential to make a substantial contribution fulfilling our vocations well into our eighties and even beyond.

Keep in mind, when I use the word *retirement* it is only as a retirement *to* something rather than *from* something. We retire to a new opportunity. Retirement is not an exit from but an entrance into what may be the most fruitful and satisfying chapter of our lives. It can be satisfying not so much because of the golf course and the grandkids, which can be a huge part of life, but because of the good work we will now be doing. This will require, for most if not all, an intentional move, a proactive choice, a conscious decision to let go and move into this new chapter.

But we need to make the move. Everything within us will want to cling to the security and comfort—the identity—of the labor that has defined our working lives through our fifties when we were masters of a craft and had positions of power and influence and the symbols that went with it. I think for example of the lawyer with the corner office on the sixteenth floor, a partner in the firm with a client base the longing of all junior lawyers, established, respected and starting to recognize that a transition is coming. Whether it is an internal niggling of the heart or something external in the firms or the organizations of which we are part—perhaps even a forced retirement—now is the time, the crucial time, to no longer dwell on the past but to embrace what might indeed be some of the most fruitful and vocationally rewarding years of our lives.

But it will mean letting go. For the president of the United States, there is no alternative. He or she can only stay in office for two terms. And there is no negotiation on this; no possibility at all that you can overstay or ask for one more year or just six months so you can line up your next job. You have to go. And I wonder if it is a severe mercy, meaning that it is a *mercy*. Why? Because so many overstay—particularly men who seemingly cannot let go of the visual symbols of their occupation. I will say it again: so many overstay.

In the academic world, I am amazed at how many times it comes up that someone has stayed in the presidency too long past their shelf life, past their capacity to lead effectively. We have, perhaps, inadvertently extolled long tenures—noting that so-and-so was the president for twenty or twenty-five years—as though this was inherently a good thing. But rarely if ever is it the right thing for an institution or an organization or a government leader, especially in executive responsibilities. Churches face the same issue with senior pastors who overstay.

Are their exceptions? Of course, but make it a rule of thumb and life that you will be the first, not the last, to know that it is time to go and that you will have at least two or three friends who have the courage and grace to tell you when it is time to step out of the role in which you have been serving.

Letting go means we accept that transitions are part of life. We embrace opportunities when they are given to us but then release them, recognizing that the new thing to which we are called will not emerge until we let go. And all of this is part of what it means to grow older.

It must be said, though, that none of this will happen if we think or assume that age is a curse. Few things are more crucial to life, especially as we move into our senior years, than the gracious acceptance that we are, well, *older*. The ideal, of course, is that we actually see the passing of years as a gift. Yes, a *gift*. We reject ageism. We reject crude jokes about growing older though we learn to not take ourselves too seriously (and if humor can help us grow older well, so be it). We reject degrading the dignity and glory of our senior years. Rather, we age with a deep respect for those who are older, those into whose

> Where do we see the potential to invest our time?

company we are now moving. For with the gift of age comes an opportunity to embrace a new chapter: to retire into a new opportunity.

We ask, given our history and what we have learned along the way, Where do we see the potential to invest our time? To chair the board of a nonprofit, to pour some energy into that garden out back that we have so longed to give time to, to complete that novel that we've always wanted to write, or to find huge satisfaction in teaching a Bible class at our local church? For some there will be significant continuity with what they have been doing already: a Tony Blair, for example, who leverages his experience as a prime minister of the United Kingdom to work toward advocating peace in the Middle East. And for others, there will be more discontinuity, where they leave a medical practice or managing a trucking firm and set up a studio in their home and the painting hobby now becomes no longer just a hobby but the focus of their day.

But either way, it means letting go. We do not cling to the former structures and symbols of our lives. We let go of the need to go to work each day, to an office or a role that we know is but the vestige of what it used to be, and now chart a new course that reflects the best possible focus of our creative energies.

It is crucial here, and this must be stressed, that we move into our senior years with grace and good humor. The world does not need grumpy old men and women who now have all kinds of time on their hands to criticize their successors, or to criticize the next generation. It is an understood rule of thumb in the US presidency that a former president never publicly criticizes a successor. Never. We move into our senior years as sages and elders who bless those who follow us.

And now, in our senior years, we respond to opportunities that come our way to bless the next generation, to empower those who are younger, to encourage them and, as invited (remember, no unsolicited advice!), to counsel and offer words of insight into the challenges that those who are younger might be facing.

If we are going to move into our senior years with integrity and grace, it will mean not only that we graciously accept that we are growing older, but that age is not merely a factor in our vocation but integral to our vocational identity. And this means that we actually embrace the aging process. As someone put it so well about the Canadian singer and songwriter Leonard Cohen: "He writes songs that could only be written by an old guy." That's it. We embrace our senior years not with regrets about the passing of life but eager to see what the new chapter will bring and what new possibilities emerge precisely because we are older.

THE POWER OF BLESSING

So I have spoken of three life and vocational transitions. Each is critical, requiring intentionality and purpose, thoughtful and prayerful reflection, and good conversation. Each of these is a liminal time and potentially a time of vulnerability. We need the community as an essential context for all six of the questions being considered, but likely we will feel this need most keenly—the need for the company and encouragement of others—in order to experience effective and grace-filled transitions through the stages of an adult life. Young people will be tempted to stay in the security and comfort of home

and parents. Those in mid-life will be inclined, perhaps, to
not make hard decisions and seek to enjoy the apparent
freedom of not having to focus or accept that we are not
everything we want to be. And in our senior years, the temp-
tation is so strong to cling to all that seemed important to us
in our forties and fifties, especially the symbols of prestige,
power and position. But now we venture out with the support
of friends and the encouragement of the community into new
waters. Doing so is essential to our vocational development
and essential to the wisdom of Psalm 78: the phenomenal
process, the pilgrimage of life, as we receive and welcome the
faith of our ancestors, take responsibility for our own lives and
then pass on the faith to the generation that follows us.

Notice this as well: we cannot navigate this road alone. We
need the companionship of fellow pilgrims. In particular, our
lives are deeply enriched and our vocational capacity enhanced
when we have strong and vital intergenerational connections
and relationships, when young men and women know the
blessing and encouragement of those a generation older than
themselves, not so much their parents but the peers of their
parents. And the senior years are potentially quite satisfying
precisely because of the joy that comes in being a friend and
mentor to those a generation younger. Thus, perhaps one of
the abiding evidences of strong and vital churches and congregations is that they are intergenerational communities.

Young men and women seek out and know the blessing of

their elders; they cannot grow in strength and vocational vitality without the blessing of those who are older, thinking of blessing as authorization and empowerment. So they go and they get it; they find it. And those who are older do not view themselves as critics of the next generation but as "blessers," finding ways to affirm, encourage and empower those who are younger.

I ask young men and women: Who are the older men and women in your life? As a rule, it will be gender specific. It is not that older women cannot be mentors to younger men; of course they can. And older men can be a source of blessing and wisdom to younger women. But generally the most pivotal connections will be older men to younger men and older women to younger women. How you answer this question says a lot about you, your current situation and your potential. We cannot navigate the transitions of vocation without the blessing of our seniors.

For those moving into mid-life, it is not the "general" blessing that they seek, but the specific blessing that comes from those within their chosen profession, like the laying on of hands from Paul to Timothy (2 Tim 1:6-7) or the affirmation of a young artist by a veteran who has nothing left to prove. This is the blessing of the passing on of the craft, the anointing within the guild one of those who will pick up the baton.

What Are Your Life Circumstances?

The LORD is my shepherd, I shall not want.
   He makes me lie down in green pastures;
he leads me beside still waters;
   he restores my soul.
He leads me in right paths
   for his name's sake.

Even though I walk through the darkest valley,
   I fear no evil;
for you are with me;
   your rod and your staff—
   they comfort me.

You prepare a table before me
   in the presence of my enemies;
you anoint my head with oil;

> my cup overflows.
> Surely goodness and mercy shall follow me
>   all the days of my life,
> and I shall dwell in the house of the LORD
>   my whole life long. (Ps 23)

Psalm 23 is likely the most quoted and best known of all the Psalms. With good reason: its central themes and words of assurance are a source of deep comfort and encouragement. It reminds us of the extraordinary wonder that regardless of our circumstances, we are not alone. God is with us as a good shepherd through both the good times and the dark valleys, through seasons of blessing and encouragement, and in the midst of trial, difficulty and perplexity. And we have the remarkable assurance that goodness will follow us and that the mercy of God will rest upon us regardless of our circumstances.

NAMING OUR REALITY

This assurance is vital to the process of considering our calling, because vocation is always fulfilled in a particular time and place. To use the wonderful phrase that Mordecai uses in the book of Esther to highlight the unique situation in which Esther finds herself, our vocations are always for "such a time as this" (Esther 4:14). Our vocations are always for *this* time and *this* place. Always. We always embrace the good work to which we are called in response to actual circumstances, challenges and opportunities. No one is ahead of their time; no one missed their time.

Further, this means that vocation is not generic, by which I mean that we do not fill out a form about ourselves and our interests and strengths and then turn to the back of the booklet to see if we are to be an engineer, artist or preacher. Rather, our vocations are always received and responded to in light of the *actual* situations in which we find ourselves. And typically these are circumstances over which we may have very little control. We have been placed here, in this time and place, and now we need to navigate our way through what lies before us. What must be stressed is that wise women and men refuse to think of themselves as victims of their circumstances, but rather as those who have been providentially situated—before God and in the grace of God—and will respond with courage, creativity and patience to what is at hand.

Gardeners understand this. They know that you have to work with what you are given. An examination of the soil, the weather patterns, the transition of the seasons, including the potential of a microclimate on this side of a hill or in a valley, guides them as they plant their gardens. So they ask: What can thrive *here*, in this soil, in this climate, in this time and place?

But we have to press this further and note that our circumstances can be remarkably fluid. Our world changes; our circumstances change. Integral to discerning vocation is appreciating what has changed or is changing and what it means for us, for our work and our calling. Therefore, we consider our calling in light of what is actually the case, not what we wish was the case.

This means no harking back to a previous time, a kind of nostalgia for another time and place in the past. My British friends might like to sing, "Rule Britannia! Britannia rules the waves!" That's fine with me as long as they know that in actuality Britannia does *not* rule the waves and that it has been over a century since it did. This is nothing more than nostalgia at best. Saying so makes a huge difference actually. If the United Kingdom is going to effectively navigate the global stage and act wisely on that stage, they had best have a clear sense of the actual state of affairs, not as they wish they were but as they actually are. The same applies to all countries. We live in the reality as it actually is or we do not engage our world and our circumstances well.

It is similar with a church. We can sing about "old-time religion" and hearken back to an earlier generation, perhaps to circumstances that we might think of as a golden age. But that kind of nostalgia is useless or even worse than useless. We need to name our reality—the changing social, cultural and demographic contours of our community—and then engage that reality as it *actually* is, not as we wish it were. We must celebrate pastors and lay elders who rather than bemoaning changes in the demographics of their neighborhoods instead ask, So what does this mean for our ministry today? What does the change in our context, our situation, mean for our approach to mission?

I think of mission and church agencies that for many years sent missionaries as pioneer evangelists and church planters and who persist at doing this again and again even though the global scene has changed and changed dramatically. In some contexts and settings it makes much more sense for local leadership to take the initiative. They speak the language; they do not need visas. We might reminisce of a previous era when God called western missionaries to preach the gospel to the farthest reaches of the known world. But the circumstances have changed. In a globalized world, in the case of Australia, Canada, the United Kingdom, the United States and many other nations, the world has come to us. Toronto, Vancouver, Sydney and Melbourne are the most multicultural cities in the world. Doing "mission" has changed. In fact, it needs to change for the simple reason that the world has changed.

As the president of a small university in western Canada, part of my job is to help the board and the faculty name reality: to address our actual circumstances, without blaming others or ourselves, but with clear-eyed focus. In light of changes in teaching methods, demographics, economic, cultural and social variables, we ask: What is our reality?

But the main point I am making is that this principle applies to each of us personally. What is our reality? How can we come to know how we are called now in this time and place, and in the midst of these circumstances?

We move beyond nostalgia. We avoid sentimentalizing our circumstances. And we turn from resentment that our circumstances are not as we wish they were. We take what is given us and ask what it means for the work to which we are called.

Each of our situations will have many diverse elements. We are, perhaps, married with four children, one of whom has a significant learning challenge, and perhaps also we have

> We cannot face our reality if we do not do so through the lens of the goodness and providential care of God.

parents with health challenges, and we have a mortgage and . . . and . . . and. This is always how it is: God's calling on our lives will consistently be in light of our actual circumstances.

Perhaps we're unemployed, live with the detritus of a broken marriage and with regrets that we did not spend more time in school when we were younger. But nothing is gained by any "if onlys." So now we ask—without blaming ourselves or others, without investing wasted energies in wondering what might have been—where and how is God calling us now? In the midst of this situation? Not as we wish it was, but as it *actually* is? We learn to say "it is what it is"—not in despair, not fatalistically—but with grace. We name reality.

And this is why the words of Psalm 23 are so poignant. We

cannot face our reality if we do not do so through the lens of
the goodness and providential care of God. The Psalmist reminds us that we are not engaging this situation on our own.
We can ask the hard questions about our context because we
know that God is with us, because we are confident in the
possibilities of grace in the midst of this situation and because
we know that ultimately good will triumph over evil. We
know and learn to live in this grace, that the mercy of God
does and will rest upon us.

CONSTRAINTS AND OPPORTUNITIES

One way to think about our context—our location in time—
is to see both the constraints and opportunities that mark our
situation. When we do a read of our circumstances we will
always come up against constraints, the limits that we inevitably bump up against, and opportunities of potential ways
forward from within and moving beyond our situation. Since
our situation will always be marked by both constraints and
opportunities, we can engage with a *hopeful realism*.

In both cases, we need to be clear: Are these real opportunities and are these real constraints? When the door is closed,
the door is closed. If the train has left the station then we
missed the train. Nothing is gained by wishing it otherwise
and nothing is gained by harping about it or bemoaning our
fate. Now we have to step back and consider our situation.
Without despair, we name our reality and consider our options

with all the creativity that God has given us. No illusions. No wishful thinking it was otherwise. No blaming others or ourselves. It is critical that we see things clearly, so we can and must ask: What opportunities and options are *truly* before us—real, live possibilities that arise out of our current situation? Yes, we respond with creativity and hopefulness, but it is a hopeful realism, not wishful thinking or misguided optimism.

We need to face the limits of our time and space. This is essential. But we must be alert to constraints that are only constraints in our minds. Often what we need are companions, friends and colleagues who challenge us when we overstate our limits or the limits of our situation. Sure, we have three children at home, or perhaps have a significant physical disability, or observe that we love doing interior design but do not have any formal training to do this kind of work. All legitimate observations. But in conversation with a friend, might we see windows of opportunity, ways in which we could invest our time even with these constraints? We need friends who can help us to avoid the propensity to any level of self-pity or feeling victimized by our circumstances and rather to consider: How and in what way could I be open to the possibilities of grace in this situation? We can pray the wonderful benediction found midway through the book of Ephesians: "Now to [the God] who by the power at work within us is able to accomplish abundantly far more than all we can ask or imagine . . ." (Eph 3:20). We are always attentive to the possibilities of grace, regardless of our circumstances.

And here is where so many choose to turn back again and again to Psalm 23, which testifies powerfully and evocatively to the presence and power of God in our lives. We do not walk this road alone. God is with us, even through the valley of the shadow of death. No set of circumstances we might be facing is beyond the pale of God's presence and grace. Goodness and mercy will follow us through each day of our lives.

When we speak of our circumstances, we can perhaps speak of how those who have gone before us have messed things up. Or how we, in our decisions or actions, made poor choices. We can name sin and evil; we can name our mistakes or misdeeds. That is fine. But because we are not ultimately victims of our past, and given that we know that wrong and evil and our mistakes are not the last word, we can speak of the possibilities of grace. In other words, we name reality but it is a *hopeful* reality. We see reality through the lens of the goodness and mercy of God.

Our reality might include a duty we have to family. The father of young boys recognizes the priority of those boys in his life and work. Aging parents will often shape our lives and our priorities. We name our reality and then we discern, before God, how we are being called to live within those limits, those contours that shape our lives and our commitments. And then within those limits we ask: Where is God in this and how can we appropriate the grace of God for this time and this place?

Let me also add this: it is essential that we name reality and learn to live within our situation as it actually is and not as we wish it to be, but we must not be so resigned to the social order that we fail to accept and embrace the call to make a difference. Sometimes, our social location may be one in which, as a woman, we feel we cannot accept or embrace a role because of how the social context "constrains" us. Perhaps we live with this. Or perhaps not. Perhaps we instead resolve that we will press against those limits. This is, of course, a matter of discernment: to know where God is calling us to live within constraints and when we are called to push against the status quo.

> It is essential that we name reality and learn to live within our situation as it actually is and not as we wish it to be.

In other words, we speak of constraints, but this does not mean there is never a time to challenge what are perceived to be our limits with a gracious courage, creativity and conviction. There will be opportunities when we sense the divine initiative in this situation, for this time and place. I wonder if, in some way, every calling is meant to challenge the status quo. Every calling is a "new thing" by which we are grace to these very real circumstances and constraints. We engage our circumstances with deliberation, choice and responsibility, and ask: How can I be intentional, doing the right thing to which I am called, rather than resigning myself to fate? We choose to do what needs to be done in this time and place.

And yet, while we live with a holy discontent in our circumstances, there is also a necessary call for each of us to live graciously *within* our circumstances. It is so easy to be a critic: to always see how the church where we worship is wrong about something or weak or pathetic, or how our daily work situation is flawed, or how the city where we live is poorly governed. Little if anything is gained by constantly railing against our circumstances as though we have a prophetic gift to denounce all that is wrong around us. This is not only tiresome for others; it also has an insidious effect on our own souls. Rather, we need to be alert to how improvement and growth can happen. We need to learn how to live each day grateful for what is given to us, for the privilege of working with these people, living in this town, worshipping at this church, while always attentive to the ways, big and small, where we might be invited to make a difference, to make a contribution, to be an instrument of God's goodness and mercy.

We live and work in a world that is in a state of flux, an ever-changing environment. We come up against new circumstances, new constraints and opportunities. We say, "It is what it is," and then discern our calling for such a time as this.

NO COMPARISONS

When I considered self-knowledge (question two) I emphasized the need to avoid comparisons between ourselves and others. Similarly, just as nothing is gained by constantly comparing ourselves to others—their gifts, opportunities—nothing is gained by wishing you had a different set of circumstances. Rather, wisdom calls us to see ourselves as placed in this situation, providentially by the hand of God, and we give ourselves wholeheartedly to what is before us.

We need to remember that every calling is unique. This means that even if our circumstances are relatively similar, you and I may well be called to respond differently. You may feel that you are called to move back to your home city to care for your aging parents. All good. But in similar circumstances, I may sense that I am being called to stay put and make other arrangements for the care of my parents. Your response to your circumstances does not obligate me; we each respond on our own terms.

Vocation is found at the interface of all six questions, not just the question about our circumstances. So beware of someone saying, "Well, when I was in your situation, this is what I did . . ." as though that somehow means you do not need to even ask the question of yourself, as though the hard thinking and discernment has already been done for you. We certainly do need to let others know how our experience might inform the life transitions they are facing, but we only do so as a means of providing an example of how another navigated a similar situation. And then we free the other to be who they are called to be in their context and situation.

For example, I think of two women who at similar stages of life both had to wrestle with the failing health of their mothers. Both daughters lived overseas, but one chose to resign her position, move back to her home city to live with her mother and be with her through her dying days. The other woman chose to make alternate arrangements for her mother and stay engaged in her international responsibilities. Both decisions are good and both women acted in a way that still recognized the limits that new circumstances placed upon them.

In this regard, we can free one another to act with courage, humility and discernment, recognizing that we will not all respond in the same way. Two friends might be worshiping at the same church. In light of changing circumstances one might choose to leave the church, feeling that in good conscience she has no choice but to leave. But her friend might choose to stay, just as clearly as an act of conscience. And despite their different responses to similar circumstances, both could and likely are responding in truth.

Yet the bottom line remains: we engage our circumstances through the lens of the possibilities of grace. This means that we engage our situation with joyful hope. We walk into our circumstances and through them with generosity. This hopeful realism is only possible in Christ. We see our circumstances, however difficult and overwhelming they may be, through the lens of the Christ event. We are always attentive to the possibilities of grace and we live trusting in the Lord who is our shepherd. Yes, we say "it is what it is," but then we also say, "Surely goodness and mercy shall follow me all the days of my life."

What Is the Cross
You Will Have to Bear?

Incline your ear, O LORD, and answer me,
    for I am poor and needy.
Preserve my life, for I am devoted to you;
    save your servant who trusts in you.
You are my God; be gracious to me, O Lord,
    for to you do I cry all day long.
Gladden the soul of your servant,
    for to you, O Lord, I lift up my soul.
For you, O Lord, are good and forgiving,
    abounding in steadfast love to all who call on you.
Give ear, O LORD, to my prayer;
    listen to my cry of supplication.
In the day of my trouble I call on you,
    for you will answer me. (Ps 86:1–7)

Our work is a participation in the work of God, so we have asked the question, "What on earth is God doing?" But that then leads to the "how" question: *How* is God doing this work? And this inevitably brings us to the cross of Christ Jesus.

We come to see that the cross reflects not something incidental or secondary to the ways of God, but that it is a lens into the heart of the Creator. By this I mean that the cross was not merely a clever means by which God could bring about the salvation of one and all. What must be appreciated is that the cross tells us something—or better, *reveals* something—about the very nature and ways of God.

This is why so many are taken with the opening words of Psalm 86. The words of the psalmist remind us that we can turn to God wherever and whenever and find in God one who is for us not against us. Even more, the Lord God is *inclined* (what a tremendous word!) toward us, leaning in and eager to be the One who responds to us in our time of need. The cross is the powerful revelation of this divine disposition: a demonstration that God is the Servant who gives his very self. Indeed, God gives the very Son of God for the sake of the world.

God is Creator and Redeemer, and God is powerful, no doubt. But the danger is that we are taken with and celebrate this power but miss that the very heart of God is this disposition of self-giving for the sake of others, for the sake of all humanity and for the sake of the whole cosmos. Any and all divine power is in the service of this self-giving God. It is so beautiful and so compelling that God's power finds ultimate and exquisite expression in the cross.

It is against this backdrop that we come to the extraordinary call of Jesus to his disciples:

> Then Jesus told his disciples, "If any want to become my followers, let them deny themselves and take up their cross and follow me. For those who want to save their life will lose it, and those who lose their life for my sake will find it. For what will it profit them if they gain the whole world but forfeit their life? Or what will they give in return for their life?" (Mt 16:24-26)

This suggests to us that our Christian identity and our work is infused with and animated by the paschal mystery, the way of the cross. The cross of Christ does not exempt us from our own cross but actually reveals to us the ways of God and thus the ways of those who live in intimate fellowship with God, who do their work in response to the call of God. We engage our world as those who hear the call of Christ, the One who calls and sends his disciples as the Father had sent him (Jn 20:21). Just as the cross was integral to the calling of Christ, a "cross" of some sort will intersect our lives and be integral to our vocation, the good work to which we are called.

And so it is very helpful to ask: "What is the cross that I have been called to bear?" It can be very helpful for each of us to consider this question in light of our circumstances and our calling, and how we are being invited by God to do good work. In other words, the cross of Christ will find different expressions in different people's lives. And yet there are some universal principles, some common perspectives that will shape our understanding of work and vocation.

THE MEANING OF THE CROSS: FOR THE SAKE OF OTHERS

First, the invitation to identify with the cross is a reminder that our lives are lived for the sake of others. As so powerfully demonstrated in the hymn of Philippians 2, the life and ministry of Christ was one of self-giving. The Apostle Paul uses quite stunning language in his reflections on his calling when he writes to the Corinthian believers and speaks of the depth of his desire to serve the Christians in Corinth. Clearly, he thinks of his life and his ministry as lived for the sake of others, so much so that he echoes the language of the cross, of "death is at work in us, but life in you" (2 Cor 4:12).

This way of being and seeing and responding to our world reflects the heart

> Our work will reflect the ways of God, the same God who acted through the cross of Christ Jesus.

of God. It means that we can only get a sense of the good work to which we are called if and as we align our hearts—our

disposition of heart or our inclination of heart—to the heart of
God. This is the very core of what it means to be called by God
for good work: our work will reflect the ways of God, the same
God who acted through the cross of Christ Jesus.

I once read an autobiographical reflection by a woman
thinking about her own work and vocation, and she noted that
during her college years she waited on tables at a local restaurant. She spoke of this as diaconal training. Perhaps for all
of us we should have a chapter in our lives when we are
waiting on others, attending to the immediate needs of others,
whether as waiters, cleaning staff in a hotel, taxi drivers,
plumbers fixing a broken water line for another, emergency
room nurses and paramedics, or whatever role cuts against the
grain of our hearts in our desire to be waited on and served.
We wait, notebook in hand, and ask: May I take your order?
We are servants and have a job or role where we are very
clearly serving others—where the way of humility draws us
into the way of Christ in the world. The hope, of course, is
that this would instill—habituate—within us that *all* work
done in the name of Christ is work done for the sake of others
as an act of generous service.

THE WAY OF SUFFERING

Second, the way of the cross suggests to us that the way of
suffering, failure and disappointment inevitably intersects
with our lives and our work. We cannot assume that the way

of the authentic vocation for the Christian follows the way of ease and success. There will be setbacks and failure; there will be difficulty and actual suffering. Wise Christians know and learn that this is a basic life principle. We know that difficulty will be part of the journey, so we should not be blindsided when we are hit with pain and suffering, wondering how this could ever happen to us.

The affirmation that suffering and failure will be part of our journey is never an excuse for foolish mistakes or for a lack of wisdom, excellence or attention to detail. It is rather an acknowledgment that failure and difficulty will come our way because God calls us to accept with grace the way of the cross.

We can note here that the point at which the cross intersected the life of the Apostle Paul was a means of grace for himself and for others. Not only did he speak of how death was at work in him and life was at work in others (as I have already noted), but also how the "thorn in the flesh" was a means by which he was empowered to lean into the grace of God (2 Cor 12:7-9).

For some, perhaps many, the way of the cross means a willingness to accept criticism and obscurity. The danger here is that we are tempted to dismiss or discount legitimate criticism simply because it is our "cross." And yet if we read between the lines of the Apostle Paul's autobiographical statements in 2 Corinthians, we recognize that this was likely, to some significant degree, the cross that he bore. In this epistle, he seems to speak

to this more obliquely, but at the conclusion of 1 Timothy he
is quite upfront about those who caused him much hardship
and grief.

THE CALL TO SACRIFICE

Third, to speak of the cross is a reminder to each one of us that
the calling of God, in Christ, will require sacrifice. Embracing
our vocation means accepting that there will be something we
might otherwise have—something good—that we let go.
Deep within the Christian theological tradition is the witness
of religious orders: Benedictine, Franciscan, Dominican and
others, including nineteenth- and twentieth-century Evangelical missionary organizations. At the heart of their understanding of vocation, those who joined the order or the
mission agency chose the way of poverty and celibacy (the
Catholic religious orders) or the way of simplicity, obscurity
and difficulty for their lives and ministries. They did not "give
up" wrong or evil but rather they gave up the good for the sake
of the greater good. Of course, not all are called in like manner,
but the heritage of the religious orders and these missionary
societies is a reminder that many have been called to set aside
perfectly good things for the sake of the good work—the vocation—to which they were called.

Now there are some things we cannot "sacrifice." Someone
may choose to remain celibate and single for the sake of their
vocation, but a married person does not have the option of

sacrificing the married life. If we are married, we have an obligation to our spouse. In like manner, if we have children, we have an obligation and duty to be a parent to them. A good case can also be made that we do not have the option of sacrificing our health.

Yet with these caveats, the point remains: God will call all of us in a way that invites us to see that our vocation, this calling, has a claim on our lives. The artist and the pastor and many others will recognize that in order to embrace this calling, we have to let something else go, perhaps marriage, a well-paying job or something else. Perhaps. But we willingly let go because the calling, the vocation, has a claim on our life for the simple reason that it comes from God.

RECOGNIZING THE PARTICULARITY OF OUR CROSS

Now with these three basic observations about the cross in mind, consider whether the cross you are called to bear might be *intrinsic* or *extrinsic* to your calling.

By intrinsic I mean that all who have this vocation or calling will, in a sense, bear this very cross. It goes with the job, whether the work of the scholar, social worker or politician. This discomfort or difficulty or stress is part of the job; something like, "if you don't like the heat, then perhaps you are not called to be a chef."

Don't choose to be a hockey goalie if you don't like the idea of powerful athletes firing pucks at high velocity in your direction. Or if you are not prepared to engage in hours and hours and hours of training—not pleasant training but necessary training—then perhaps you are not called to this profession since this goes with the territory.

Don't be a pastor if you are simply not prepared to graciously accept the dynamics of church politics. It goes with the territory!

Don't go into business if you are not prepared to live with and work within the vagaries of the economy. And if you become a politician, accept that whether you like it or not, you are vulnerable to the moods of those who vote for or do not vote for your party. That's life in the political world.

Other times the cross is *extrinsic*, meaning it is unique to the way in which you, in particular, might be called to be a pastor, artist, athlete or plumber. Perhaps you are a single mother and have to navigate the care of two small children while constantly scrambling to negotiate the demands of your day job. Perhaps you have a physical ailment or disability. Perhaps as a doctor you sense a calling to work with Doctors Without Borders among the refugees in a war zone. Perhaps as an artist, you lack any level of encouragement or support from your spouse or religious community.

Regardless of whether it is intrinsic or extrinsic to the particular work to which we are called, the bottom line remains the same: the cross of Christ intersects our lives, and the genius of a Christian perspective on vocation is that we accept this and bear this with grace, patience and humility. This is not something about which we are constantly complaining, but something we carry quietly. The great danger is that the cross would be a weight on our lives and our spirits, and that we would lose our capacity for joy, for love and generosity and compassion toward others.

We do not and should not broadcast this. We do not need to. I do not need to be constantly mentioning my cross. Maybe, actually, I should never talk about it except with my most intimate friends. But even at home, my wife does not need me coming home every day and be-

> When we follow Christ we learn the way that leads to life.

moaning my cross and making this the topic of conversation at the dinner table day in and day out. Those who are close to us likely know where the cross intersects our lives; no doubt it comes up in our conversations from time to time. But the tone and character of our days is shaped by joy, not by a continual "woe is me." As the Apostle Paul observes in 2 Corinthians 7:4, in all of his troubles he was nevertheless overjoyed.

But why bother? Who needs this?

Why would anyone willingly take up a cross? Well, here is a way we can think about this. Imagine a varsity volleyball coach recruiting potential top players for her team that she fully expects will contend in the coming season. She makes it very clear: We want you on the team, but it will be hard slugging. You will be up and on the practice court every day at 6 a.m. for a grueling hour of drills. No let up; no compromise. You either suck it up or you do not make the team. If you make the team, you join a winner. We will contend for the league championship. It will not be easy, but will it be worth it? Of course it will. You are going to be part of a winning team.

Jesus himself endured the cross for the joy that was set before him (Heb 12:2). In other words, the cross was nothing compared to the big picture—the reward. And in like manner, he asks us to be part of carrying the pain of this world. It will not be easy. It will call for our deepest reserves, our greatest patience and a capacity for endurance. It will press us to the limit but it will be worth it. When we follow Christ we learn the way that leads to life. And the pain, while real, is secondary to the prize that awaits us.

I remember a conversation in which I was seeking to persuade someone to truly consider accepting a position he had been offered. After much conversation back and forth, in response to my acknowledgment that there was a side of that job that would be difficult, he said, "But Gordon, that is simply not my cross."

I realized right away that he was right. It was not his cross. Sometimes, of course, we have no choice: we have a speech impediment or other disability or something else in our circumstances around which we have no choice. It is what it is. But at other times we are wise to ask, Is this the cross that God has asked me to bear? Nothing is gained by being heroic or embracing a false sense of martyrdom. Rather, we assume responsibilities and opportunities with our eyes open and alert to the ways in which God is actually inviting us into the way of the cross. My friend was more than willing to bear a cross. That was not the issue. The issue was the fundamental character of *his* calling. We have to be alert to those pressure points in our religious communities that might urge us to sacrifice that which we have no business sacrificing. This is another form of a false cross.

Our Baptismal Identity and the Sign of the Cross

All this is a reminder that our vocations are a vital means by which we fulfill our baptismal identity. Baptism is a mark, a kind of tattoo on our lives, a symbol even more powerful and significant than the ring on the fourth finger of my left hand. Our vocation is now part of what it means to live in a way consistent with the meaning of our baptism, under the mercy of God, with ultimate allegiance to no other agency, authority, clan or nation than Christ. As the baptized, Christ has prior claim on our lives and prior claim on how we engage the world of our work, career and vocation. Through baptism, we are united with Christ in his death (Rom 6) and embrace the

way of death and self-denial, knowing we will have the grace
to rise with him.

By virtue of our baptisms, we choose the way of the cross.
Our vocations, our work in the world, are done under the *sign*
of the cross. I come from a religious heritage that feels some
ambivalence about the cross that might hang from the mirror
of the taxi, or the act of signing the cross for the soccer player
who has just been substituted into a match. I get it; it seems
routine, ritualistic and almost superstitious. And yet I wonder
if another perspective might be that we should all go about our
work—whether in the garden or the lecture hall, at the nurses'
station or the art studio—under the sign of the cross. Perhaps
the sign of the cross is precisely that which physically and tan-
gibly draws us in our bodies to the very identification that we
long for, that our work would be done in the name of Christ.

The signing of the cross is actually quite an ancient practice.
Fourth-century theologian St. John Chrysostom urged:
"Never leave home without making the sign of the cross." Is
there wisdom here? With each transition, even the everyday
transitions that take us to the marketplace, to schools, to carpenter workshops, might we go under the cross and do
whatever we can to keep this in mind? Some may choose to
make this entirely an inward and internal matter, a quiet
thought or mental note to self that "I am doing this under the
cross." And that is fine. But some may actually choose to express it physically in the same way that a person might kneel

for prayer or raise one's hands in worship. Others might also choose to go into their place of work with a quietly expressed sign of the cross over their forehead, heart, lips and hands. The preacher heads into the pulpit with the sign of the cross, signaling to self and to all that this is an act of identification with the cross of Christ. The pilot settles into the cockpit making the sign of the cross. The surgeon, heading into the operating room. The plumber considering the challenge of a major blockage. Why not? When I see a soccer player head onto the pitch with the sign of the cross, it can be a reminder to me that whenever I enter into the playing field to which I am called, it is fitting that I take on this work under the cross of Christ.

SUFFERING AND THE LIFE OF THE CHURCH

Finally, our preaching and teaching within the context of the church needs to regularly highlight that the way of the cross and the way of suffering are inherent to our Christian experience. Beware of those Christian communities that suggest that if one has sufficient faith, suffering will be a thing of the past. What is urgently needed are not nice, sentimental songs about how everything goes well if we just trust Jesus or simplistic preaching and teaching that bypasses the reality of suffering in our lives.

Rather, we need communities of faith that speak of the way of the cross as part of the natural course of our liturgies, our music and our teaching. We can sing "It is Well with My

Soul," with its extraordinary and breathtaking line: "When sorrows like sea billows roll." We can and must preach those texts of Scripture that remind us that difficulty, setback and disappointment bring us into deeper fellowship with Christ; we are joint heirs with him in his suffering (Rom 8:17). These themes in our worship and preaching can empower us to accept the cross graciously, reminding us that our deepest longing is not a life of ease, but a life of greater union with and identification with Christ.

And more, when it comes to empowering one another to embrace our respective vocations, we can call to mind the words of 2 Timothy 2:3: "Share in suffering like a good soldier of Christ Jesus." The Apostle seems to be suggesting here that suffering will be part of the character and contours of the work to which Timothy is called. Timothy needed to be bolstered and encouraged—affirmed, lest he think abnormal any suffering he might experience—to walk the way of the cross with grace, courage and patience.

When we speak of the cross, it is imperative we affirm that the cross we bear draws us closer to Christ. More, that in the darkness and difficulty we can turn to God and pray, in the words of Psalm 86:1, "Incline your ear, O LORD, and answer me . . ."

Question Six

What Are You Afraid Of?

I lift up my eyes to the hills—
  from where will my help come?
My help comes from the LORD,
  who made heaven and earth.

He will not let your foot be moved;
  he who keeps you will not slumber.
He who keeps Israel
  will neither slumber nor sleep.

The LORD is your keeper;
  the LORD is your shade at your right hand.
The sun shall not strike you by day,
  nor the moon by night.

The LORD will keep you from all evil;
  he will keep your life.

The LORD will keep
> your going out and your coming in
> from this time on and forevermore. (Ps 121)

There are many unknowns in life. This is patently clear again and again when we face vocational transitions. We cannot see around the bend in the road. We make decisions about our lives with implications for the lives of those we love and those for whom we have some responsibilities, and there are so many unknown variables. But there is one key variable that can be a known factor in our lives:

The LORD will keep
> your going out and your coming in
> from this time on and forevermore. (Ps 121:8)

On this we can depend. It will be the same now and for each transition of our lives. If we believe this, it will be evident because fear will no longer co-opt our lives.

FEAR AND VOCATION

In the fascinating exchange between Jesus and Martha, Martha expressed frustration that her sister Mary was in-attentive to the work she was doing. Jesus' response to Martha was, "Martha, Martha, you are worried and distracted by many things" (Lk 10:41).

It is a telling observation. What many recognize, indeed

most of those who comment on or write on the topic of vocation, is that the most pressing question about us may well be, "What are you afraid of?" What are the worries and distractions that swirl around your heart and mind, keeping you from your life and work and dissipating your energies? And what are the fears that distract you and keep you from intentional focus on the good work to which you are called?

Could it be that Martha was confused about her own calling and inclined to complain to Jesus about Mary not because there was an issue with Mary as much as an issue of Martha's fear, worry and anxiety? It may well be that this final question is also the most pressing, and that the greatest obstacle to the fulfillment of our vocation is not external but internal.

Typically, we do look elsewhere—to circumstances that seem to limit our options, or to others, be they parents, potential employers or institutions—to identify what appears to be an obstacle, problem or impediment to our capacity to embrace the call of God on our lives. We often feel frustrated by others or by our circumstances, and we are inclined to assign blame to these external factors that seem to be impeding us.

But could it be that the greatest obstacle to the fulfillment of our vocation is not "out there" but rather "in here"? In our own hearts? Could the real question be not who or what is standing in our way, but, "What are you afraid of?" What is the fear that keeps us from embracing that to which God is calling us?

Wise women and men know that we are best served when we acknowledge our fears: name them, get them out on the table, consider what they mean and where they come from and then see how our lives are lived most freely when these fears do not have a controlling influence.

But this is easier said than done, because we live in a culture of fear. Fear shapes the political, economic, social and educational fabric of our societies. We live in a culture that assumes that fear, worry and anxiety are how one lives. And if you are not worried, then you simply don't care. So to care about your children, your friends, your church and your country is to worry.

We go about our work and the routine of our lives without a conscious thought about fear. We have become so habituated to our fears and worries and anxieties that we just assume this is how life is to be lived. To be alive and engaged in life and work and relationships is to be worried about life and work and relationships, as well as about our financial well-being and the future.

Do we even know what it would feel like to live in the full force of what Jesus calls us to when he very simply says, "Do not worry about your life" (Lk 12:22)? Jesus goes on to stress that worry is useless and, more to the point, inconsistent with our knowledge of God as the One who is providentially present to each one of us. But we still worry. And my point here is that we cannot assume that this fear is a secondary or inconsequential matter. It *does* matter, and we need to consider what it means for our vocations.

Let's approach this question of fear through the lens of your childhood home and consider this: Was your home a place of security, confidence and peace? Or was it marked by anxiety, worry and fretfulness? The key variable, of course, is your parents, notably the parent who was the primary caregiver for you as a child. Did your parents rest in the providential care of God, confident in the goodness of the Creator? If not, then I suggest you need to be particularly vigilant to the movements of your heart; the road will be that much more challenging for you. The impact of our parental home can be very significant and formative.

What this suggests for all of us is that we need to be deliberate, honest about our fears and intentional in considering how they might

> Worry is useless and inconsistent with our knowledge of God as the One who is providentially present to each one of us.

shape our response to our circumstances, our opportunities, our sense of what God is doing in the world and how we might respond. We need time and space for good conversation with another who can ask us the question: What are you afraid of?

What *are* you afraid of? And what kinds of questions might help us get our fears and worries out in front of us where we can talk about them?

Some fear financial loss or insecurity. We live in a culture that preaches the gospel of economic security—which may well be an oxymoron—and that a life well-lived is a life of growing assets and a secure retirement, so much so that it would seem that the only reason for living and working is to guarantee that our senior years are "safe." But even young people will often hesitate to wade out into the waters of life because they fear the vulnerability when they no longer have the backstop of their parents' financial resources. Or those in midlife cannot do the right thing because all they see are the economic implications of their decisions.

For others, there is the fear of criticism or failure, the lack of validation, or the disappointment of parents or others who matter to us. Perhaps as a child it was virtually impossible to please your parents or to know the affirmation that every child must know to be able to take risks, knowing that failure is only a bump in the road and an opportunity for new learning. A perfectionist parent almost inevitably results in a young person who is hesitant to step out and try something new.

Others fear they will be ignored and live in obscurity, that their lives will be lived in the shadows. As we get older, we fear that no one will take us seriously anymore, that a loss of physical strength will be matched by a loss of influence. If our church community and our country matter to us, we would like to think our voice and our vote make a difference, and that our influence can either sustain the good or bring about something even better.

We fear that if we are no longer in control, no longer respected and heard, that we will lose our capacity to shape future outcomes. But while those who are older might most obviously fear the loss of influence, all too easily it can catch up with us in our younger adult and mid-adult years as well. And this often means that we are grasping for roles or responsibilities that will bring us attention, affirmation and hopefully the level of influence to make us feel that our lives have significance.

Still others fear that the passing of time will happen so quickly—the clock is ticking—that their lives and opportunities will pass them by. Ironically the very fear that time is passing does not empower them to act but actually leaves them caught, frozen and unable to act. Some need deadlines to achieve their goals, but for others the deadline looms, and we freeze up, fearing failure or simply plagued by the passing of time. With the ticking clock marking off the shortness of our lives, we don't live in the moment but fear the loss of our lives.

We worry about our own lives and then all these fears are compounded when we have children or when our parents get older. In time we find that we get to worrying about our grandchildren as well.

I could go on. But the point is not so much *what* it is that we fear but rather this: Are we willing to acknowledge our fears, to name them and then learn to live in such a way that those fears do not co-opt our lives? Indeed, it is very possible that our fears will never be entirely dissipated. Not until we meet Christ face-to-face. But in the meantime, we can learn to live in freedom from the insidious power of fear.

ADDRESSING OUR FEARS

I suggest three spiritual practices that can help us to live in freedom from fear. First, we need to *name the fears* that so easily haunt us. Be intentional: get out a piece of paper and actually write them down. What fears, anxieties and points of worry or concern are circulating around your mind and heart at this time, in these circumstances, and with this choice before you and the five questions we have already considered?

I find it helpful to take up my spiritual journal and enumerate the fears, anxieties and worries—to actually put pen to paper and list them—and have them out there where I can see them in black and white.

This requires emotional honesty, of course. Without forthrightness about our fears, nothing is gained. To the contrary, they can have an unwitting influence and in some cases a control over us. The power of fear is diminished by the simple act of naming, the acknowledgment that the fear exists. Then in the liberating call of Peter, cast your cares on God, the God who cares for you (1 Pet 5:7).

When the list is complete, I have found it helpful to go back and identify what seems to me to be the deepest fear. As best as I can, I identify the greatest source of anxiety and worry in my life. It has been observed that our point of deepest fear is the point of our deepest vulnerability to evil. There is a simple power in naming this deep fear. In particular, there is power in identifying the fear that may be keeping me from engaging the good work to which I am called. So I ask: What is the most pressing fear when I consider the vocational or potential job transition situation that is before me?

Second, there is tremendous value in *conversation* with a trusted friend. One of the signs that we have a good friend—a true friend—is that we feel safe enough to discuss our fears. This reflection with another about our fear brings that fear into the light. In the light we can speak about it and receive the grace of encouragement from our friend. This sets up one of the most crucial gifts of a friendship: mutual encouragement.

I ache for those—so frequently the older men in our society—who move into their senior years without the gift of friendship and good conversation. They have never learned the essential value of grace-filled, honest conversation about joy and sorrow and, most crucially, the fears that so easily entangle us. Start young, I say, start young! In your thirties, if not earlier, cultivate friendships that will sustain you through life and work, friendships where you know the gift and grace of good conversation.

And third, there is no doubting the power of *worship*—the liturgy of the gathered people of God—where we celebrate the Christ who sits on the throne of the universe. The power of worship is not that occasionally we gather with the people of God and affirm that God is good and that God cares for his people. Rather, the formative power of worship is found in its regularity: week in and week out, we attend together to the Word and gather together at the table.

But more, there are few things so formative to our prayers and our worship as the Old Testament Psalms. Whether said or sung, the Psalms draw us to the very words that help us pray. So when we hear

> God is our refuge and strength,
>> a very present help in trouble.
> Therefore we will not fear. (Ps 46:1-2)

we are offered the confidence we need from God who cares for us. When we read

> The LORD will keep
>> your going out and your coming in. (Ps 121: 8)

we are drawn into the wonder of a God who watches over us. And if we are restless or sleepless, we hear

> I will both lie down and sleep in peace;
>> for you alone, O LORD, make me lie down in safety.
>> (Ps 4:8)

and can be reassured and comforted by God's watchful care. And in the words of Psalm 4:8, we remember that at night we can lie down and sleep in peace.

While it is often specific Psalms that draw us into this grace—the confidence that God is present to us—my point is more that the liturgy and worship of which I speak is worship that is *infused* with the Psalms. And what we learn in our bodies is that we can pray the Psalms, but more, learn to lean into the God who is revealed to us through the Psalms. We pray them again and again in our daily prayers and in our Sunday worship with our fellow believers.

In the end, we do not need worship that panders to our feelings. Rather, we need worship that very simply and consistently draws us into the presence of the God who is revealed to us through the whole of Scriptures and particularly through the Psalms.

And in all of this, preaching matters a great deal. I say to preachers, when you open the Word each week keep this in mind: your hearers' greatest need is to grow in faith, to allow the Word to strengthen their hearts, face their fears honestly and to be encouraged for the life and work to which they are called.

What is the evidence that these practices—listing our fears, conversation with another and worship informed by the Psalms—are bearing fruit, that they make any difference? What is the evidence that the power of fear is being diminished?

The evidence, quite simply, is joy. When we are freed from fear, we are empowered to live and to engage the good work to which we are called *with joy*.

Conclusion

We ask the questions, but at some point we need to make some decisions. We need to act with grace, courage and generosity. And within all the limits of what we know and what we do not know, we choose. Even with the unknowns, choices have to be made. It is my prayer that as you have considered the six questions, you have felt empowered to not only ask these questions and have the conversations, but also to act. Life is complicated and messy, but under the providential care of God we can navigate the inevitable transitions of our lives, and hopefully do it in a way that witnesses to God's goodness.

As we make the transition from conversation to action, from thinking and talking about our lives to actually living our lives, I have some concluding observations and comments to offer.

COMMUNITY

I have spoken to this priority at points along the way, but it should be explicit: we cannot effectively address any of these questions on our own. We need the grace of good, clear, honest conversation, without flattery or cliché. We need to be in conversation with women and men, both the community of peers and those older than ourselves, where our conversation can draw us into the six questions I have spoken of:

- Conversations that are intellectually challenging, challenging our vision for the work of God as we reflect on what God is doing in our world

- Conversations that are safe places for self-discovery, without flattery, but with genuine affirmation that helps give us clarity about our identity

- Conversations that affirm our life stage, with peers but also older men and women who bless us through the transitions of an adult life

- Conversations that help us name our reality clearly and confidently; shared reflections that are hope-filled and keep us from feeling sorry for ourselves, empowering us to see the possibilities of grace

- Conversations where we have a safe place to talk about the trials of life

- Conversations where we are able to talk about more than just our hopes and dreams, but also about our fears

At the very least, you should have three significant conversation partners in your life. The ideal is two peers, one of whom is perhaps within your line of work and the other who is a friend and conversation partner, but sees your life and work from another occupation or vantage point. I think here of the pastor who is in intentional conversation with one peer who is a fellow pastor and another peer who is in business. And then we should have at least one person who is a generation older than ourselves. These partners engage in conversation that helps us navigate all six of these questions, fostering good thinking and discernment.

THE MINISTRY OF THE HOLY SPIRIT

We need to affirm and confirm that the Christian vocation is fulfilled in response to and in the power and grace of the Holy Spirit. We do not live self-constructed lives. Instead, we live by intentional attentiveness to the Holy Spirit who

- illumines our minds to see and appreciate what God is doing in the world and to see the world as God sees it;

- graces us to see ourselves in truth and know the humility of self-acceptance;

- guides us through the transitions of our lives;

- strengthens us in the midst of our actual circumstances to
  see our reality with hope;

- comforts and strengthens us through the trials of life and
  work; and

- encourages us to live in hope and courage in the midst of
  our fears.

It is the Spirit who empowers, comforts and encourages us. It is the Spirit that gives us insight, wisdom, understanding and discernment to do our work well. In the end, vocation is a matter of obedience: we embrace what it is that the Spirit is calling us to do. When all is said and done, all the questions discussed, obedience is not secondary, but the heart of the matter. We do not live self-constructed lives, but lives of radical dependence on the Spirit of God who, in the words of the Nicene Creed, is the Lord and Giver of Life.

LEARNING AND PARTNERSHIPS

Consider two more questions. It is somewhat tempting to list these as questions seven and eight, but in reality they are two questions that emerge from what is distilled through honest reflection on the six critical questions I have profiled.

First, what is the new learning to which you are being called? What I find is that through each critical transition, there is new learning that is essential if we are going to move into a new stage and phase of life and work. We must be always learning, not just when we are young or only when we are getting started, but as a way of being. We read and learn; we attend seminars and we keep learning. We are in conversation with our peers, eagerly taking notes and reflecting on what we are hearing for our own situation. We learn by reading, by observation, by trial and error, but we are always learning. Even when we move into our senior years we can ask: What new learning is called for so that I can be all that I am called to be as I embrace the good work that will mark this chapter of my life?

And second, what is the critical partnership you will need to form and cultivate? An athlete needs a trainer; an artist needs an art gallery; a writer needs an editor. A nonprofit executive director needs a finance officer and board members and donors. Those called into pastoral leadership need a sponsoring denomination or church affiliation. An entrepreneur needs capital and someone to market the product or service. No one can navigate this world without others who partner with them along the way.

OBEDIENCE

Finally we come to the bottom line: the call of God is the call of God. The only reasonable response is that we accept the call. We obey.

What we learn is that obedience does not limit freedom; quite the contrary, obedience makes freedom possible. If we are airplane pilots, we don't insist on our "freedom" but rather we obey the rules of flight. The airplane soars when we submit to the principles that govern the way that flying machines take to the skies. Obedience is wisdom; we are freed—liberated—to fly.

The same principle applies to all regardless of our vocation. When we hear and respond to the call of God, it is an act of freedom; we are "free" in Christ. We learn to accept the constraints of our lives (we cannot be just anything that we want to be), and when we defer to the divine call within these constraints, we find joy, freedom and wisdom.

I think of the Annunciation—the call to Mary given through the angel Gabriel—and her stunning response: "Here am I, the servant of the Lord; let it be with me according to your word" (Lk 1:38).

As I write these words, I have before me a photograph of the painting by Caravaggio, *The Calling of St Matthew*, which hangs in San Luigi dei Francesi church in Rome. Caravaggio was a master of light and did extraordinary things with hands. In this case the hand of Christ, mirrored in the hand of St. Peter, calls to Matthew, beckoning him to come. And the issue at stake is rather simple: Will he come? Will he obey? Will he respond to the divine summons?

There will come a time in our process of vocational discernment when we can say enough is enough. We have thought through the issues and wrestled with the pros and cons. We have worked through excuses, fears, obstacles, problems and who knows what else. Now we need to accept this vocation and do what we are called to do: the good work to which we are called.

Appendix

A Prayer for Those Who Work

[for use in corporate worship]

Dear God,

We give you thanks for the gift of work—good work, by which we can honor you, serve others and provide for our basic needs.

We celebrate that we are created in your image and that you have given us talent, capacity, intelligence and opportunity to make a difference and contribute to the well-being of your world.

We give you thanks for the many people who serve us through their work, providing for our needs, enriching our lives and making our world a better place to live. And we pray for them.

We pray—

For those called into business of the production of goods and services. We thank you for how they meet our needs and we ask that they would be encouraged in their work and empowered to work with integrity, financial acumen and accountability, a commitment to excellence, and justice for all.

In your mercy,

hear our prayer.

For teachers and educators, trainers and coaches. We thank you for these gifts of those who teach and train and equip us and our children, and ask that you would give them patience, diligence, a love for truth and a love for people.

In your mercy,

hear our prayer.

For students, who in their work pursue truth, understanding and wisdom; may they delight in learning and be open and attentive and able to embrace new ideas, insights and skills and in their learning grow in wisdom and the love of God.

In your mercy,

hear our prayer.

For artists—musicians, painters, sculptors, poets, novelists, filmmakers, actors, storytellers, dancers, designers and gardeners. Grant them, we pray, a love for beauty and truth, and give them creativity, skill and depth and breadth of imagination as you keep them ever hopeful and alive to the possibilities of grace in themselves and others.

In your mercy,

hear our prayer.

For entertainers—musicians who help us dance, comedians who make us laugh, athletes who give us something to cheer for—that they might entertain with a vision for the good, the noble, the excellent and the honorable.

In your mercy,

hear our prayer.

For those in the medical professions—doctors, pharmacists, surgeons, paramedics, chiropractors, dentists, hygienists and nurses—that they might have skill, diligence and patience in their work, attending to the sick and ailing with compassion as those who serve in the name of the great Physician.

In your mercy,

hear our prayer.

For those in government—politicians and those in civil service in the various offices and branches of government, both local and federal and on a state and provincial level—that they would serve with honor, generosity and a deep and abiding commitment to the greater good in justice and fairness to all.

In your mercy,

hear our prayer.

For those who protect us and sustain and advocate for our laws and keep order and peace and maintain justice—the police, coast guard, prison officials, firefighters along with lawyers and judges—that you would keep them safe, and give them a deep patience and an abiding love for both truth and justice and a capacity for compassion in the midst of all the pressures they face.

In your mercy,

hear our prayer.

For scholars and scientists, philosophers, behavioral scientists and historians—those who foster depth and breadth of understanding and enrich our minds, equipping us to grow in wisdom—that they would be wise, skilled in research, committed to the truth and able to find the time and space to do their work well.

In your mercy,

hear our prayer.

For architects and builders—those who design our homes, schools, churches, places of work and our parks; those who actually build them, the engineers, carpenters, electricians and plumbers; and those who attend to their maintenance and repair—that they would design and build with a commitment to quality, economy and beauty, and a concern for our environment.

In your mercy,

hear our prayer.

For social workers, counselors, peacekeepers, environmental activists, prophets and diplomats—all of those who attend to our personal mental health and to our social and political networks that we would live in peace. Grant them all a capacity for discernment, compassion and love as they equip us to live at peace with ourselves and with others.

In your mercy,

hear our prayer.

For homemakers—those who create and maintain the spaces in which we live—and those who care for children. Grant them skill in their work, patience through the course of their days, a capacity for hospitality and the embodiment of the love of God as their families come and go.

In your mercy,

hear our prayer.

For those who serve in the financial sector—bankers, accountants, financial advisors and insurance brokers—that they might serve with a care for detail and accuracy but also justice, hope and integrity.

In your mercy,

hear our prayer.

For journalists, newspaper and media editors, producers and publishers—including those in marketing and advertising—who enrich our lives with great literature, including essays and opinion pieces with insight into our world and recent happenings, that they would write and publish and edit with skill and an interest in the truth, avoiding the sensational but attentive to what fosters understanding.

In your mercy,

hear our prayer.

For those in the service sector—airline pilots, flight attendants, taxi drivers, bus drivers and the mechanics who attend to the airplanes, the buses and taxis and all those who support them—for care in their work, patience with people who are impatient and a generosity of spirit as they go through their day.

In your mercy,

hear our prayer.

For farmers and all who work the land, including orchardists and winemakers, who provide food for our table, bringing in the harvest that you provide—that they would serve with an awareness of the bounty of the earth and a genuine regard for caring for the earth and its resources.

In your mercy,

hear our prayer.

For those in the hospitality industry—hotels and restaurants—where we stay when we are away from home, and where we find nourishing meals when we are not eating at home, for a spirit of generosity and hospitality to mark their work, and patience and diligence and good will, particularly for those who clean rooms and wait on tables.

In your mercy,

hear our prayer.

For those who serve in nonprofit agencies that respond to those in critical need—the homeless, the refugee, the orphaned and addicted—that they would serve with skill, insight, courage and compassion.

In your mercy,

hear our prayer.

For pastors, preachers and missionaries, and all who provide pastoral care and serve through the ministry of the Word, that they would teach with insight and courage, with compassion and anointing of the Spirit, as they draw us into fellowship with Christ, and equip us through their ministry to fulfill our God-given vocations through their teaching and encouragement.

In your mercy,

hear our prayer.

And for those who do not have gainful employment and for those whose work is a source of deep and oppressive stress, or those who cannot work because of illness, physical limitation or addiction—that they would know your presence and encouragement and ways in which, even in their limitations, they can be of service to others.

In your mercy,

hear our prayer.

Thank you for each one. And for one and all, may we each do the good work to which we are called with skill, diligence, integrity, creativity and generosity. May the anointing of the Holy Spirit rest upon each one and empower each one to do their work "as unto the Lord."

We ask all of this in the name of the Father, the Son and the Holy Spirit,

Amen.

ALSO AVAILABLE FROM GORDON T. SMITH

Called to Be Saints

Courage & Calling

Spiritual Direction

Listening to God in Times of Choice

Beginning Well

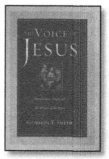
The Voice of Jesus